PREPARE WITH HONOR

PREPARE WITH HONOR

HELPS FOR FUTURE MISSIONARIES

RANDY L. BOTT

Deseret Book Company
Salt Lake City, Utah

Library of Congress Cataloging-in-Publication Data

Bott, Randy L., 1945–
    Prepare with honor: helps for future missionaries / Randy L. Bott.
        p.   cm.
    Includes bibliographical references and index.
    Summary: Provides practical advice for young men and woman, ages twelve and older, planning to serve full-time missions in the future for The Church of Jesus Christ of Latter-day Saints.
    ISBN 0-87579-954-X (pbk.)
    1. Missionaries—Juvenile literature.   2. Church of Jesus Christ of Latter-day Saints—Missions—Juvenile literature.   3. Mormon Church—Missions—Juvenile literature.   [1. Missionaries.   2. Church of Jesus Christ of Latter-day Saints—Missions.   3. Mormon Church—Missions.]   I. Title.

BX8661.B68   1995
266'.9332—dc20   95-35451
                                                                               CIP
                                                                               AC

Printed in the United States of America   71976-2769A
Profile Media, Inc., Provo, UT

10   9   8   7   6   5   4

To my children who are preparing to serve—
Mindy, Ryan, T.J., and Landon—
and to the thousands of young men and women
who are serious about making their full-time missions
some of the greatest years of their lives

Contents

CONTENTS

Preparing with Honor

Serving a full-time mission will be one of the most rewarding and difficult experiences of your life. You should be congratulated on being worthy to be considered for service. As a mission president, I watched many groups of missionaries come to our mission. During the three years my wife and I presided over the mission, more than six hundred young men and women joined us in service. On the day each of them arrived, nervous excitement filled the air. The long-awaited moment had come: the first day of their mission. At this point new missionaries realize that more diligent preparation would have been helpful. Consequently, I have written this book to help you better prepare for "the hour of your mission" (D&C 31:3).

To set the stage for the chapters that follow, let me tell a boyhood story and compare it to missionary preparation.

We were as tough as they came. In just a couple of weeks, we would be graduating from the eighth grade and would soon be off to high school. One day during music time, the teacher thrilled the boys by announcing that the freshman football coach was coming to talk to all who wanted to try out for the team in the fall. Gladly, every boy in class joined the mass exit into the gym.

We sat noisily on the floor, poking and jabbing each

other. Suddenly, a mountain of a man entered the gym. He had on a T-shirt with the high school logo imprinted on the back. He was wearing sweatpants, gym shoes, and a baseball hat, and a whistle hung from his neck. He paced in front of us until we were quiet, squarely faced us, and announced, "Men, if you want to play high school football, there are a few things I want you to do." He then outlined some basic conditioning techniques, cautioning us against eating too much candy and drinking too much pop. He also told us to run every day and ride our bikes as often as possible. He even suggested lifting weights and getting jobs that required discipline, strength, and stamina. He talked of the fun and thrill of playing and winning but reminded us that our opponents wanted to win as well. The meeting didn't last long, but were we pumped! I don't think most of us heard much past the word *men*.

As you might guess, the coach's counsel went unheeded during the much-anticipated summer vacation. Before I knew it, the summer was over. Then I received a letter explaining when and where to pick up my football gear. On a hot August afternoon, a rough-looking group of kids appeared at the gym door. We were given the old varsity gear, which had long since served its useful purpose. The shoulder pads could easily accommodate two kids, and the knee pads in the pants acted as shin guards for most of us. I could even turn my helmet a full 360 degrees without having it touch my ears. But we were tough, and we were ready to receive the trophy for Best Freshman Football Team in the State.

We were ordered onto the field to warm up by knocking shoulder pads with each other. It felt sort of funny but good. We were then assigned positions according to size and to where we happened to be standing. We were taught a few plays that we practiced for about thirty minutes. The weather was hot, and we were all thirsty. The coach blew the whistle, and we all lined up on the goal line. We expected a short pep talk, then the welcome coolness of the showers. We were mistaken. He said, "When I blow the whistle, you run full speed down to the twenty-yard line and line up there." We didn't see much sense in that, but we all obeyed anyway. At the twenty-yard line, he blew the whistle again and had us run back to the goal line. Now things were getting ridiculous. Why would he want us to just run back and forth?

On the second sprint, several of my friends ran off to the side, ripped off their helmets, and started throwing up. I guess the combination of heat, physical exertion, and poor physical condition took its toll. I laughed to myself. On the way back from the twenty-yard line, several more dropped out. On the next trip to the twenty-yard line, I started feeling sick. More dropped out. On the way back to the goal line, I dropped out and joined my friends.

The coach called us all together and sternly chewed us out for not taking seriously his challenge to prepare. He informed us that we would meet at six the next morning for a three-hour workout and then run some more wind sprints. Several kids muttered unmentionable words under their breath and assured him they wouldn't be there. They walked to the locker room and turned in their gear. No glory for them.

True to his word, we started practice at six the next morning. Although it wasn't as hot as the day before, most of us had lost our breakfast by the end of practice—including me, about halfway through the wind sprints. About six or seven boys walked off the field when the coach announced that we would meet again at 4:30 that afternoon for another practice session. Turning in their equipment, they told us how stupid we were to put up with such nonsense. They challenged us all to boycott the practice and show the coach a thing or two. We declined.

The afternoon practice was terrible. Several times, I entertained thoughts of quitting. All my muscles were sore, even some I didn't know I had. My feet were blistered, my head was pounding, my back was aching, and my hands and arms were bruised from tackling and blocking. I was in a world of hurt. More than half the team quit that afternoon.

The next morning, we were wondering if the coach was trying to kill us. We decided among ourselves that we were as tough as he was and would not give up, no matter what. No one dropped out after that. The soreness was gone after about a week, and practices started to be fun. Our anticipation of the first game greatly increased our excitement. By the end of the season, we determined that the coach was right—football *was* fun! We were the mighty freshman football team, and our motto became No Guts, No Glory.

The lessons I learned from this experience also apply to preparing for a mission. Too many young men and women seem to think all they have to do is show up and they will be prepared to serve. They are cautioned and urged and warned by loving parents, teachers, and leaders. They are given opportunities to speak in church, to ask questions in Sunday School classes, and to study in seminary. They are lovingly watched over by priesthood and Young Women leaders who emphasize the need to avoid the deceptive activities that Satan makes look so enticing. Some fall into the devilish trap of thinking, "I can sin now, then clean up my act just before I go, and everything will be all right." What a tragic misunderstanding!

The excitement is high when the call arrives. Everybody talks about where you are going and what it will be like. Girls swoon as the newly called missionaries begin their preparation. The farewell may make you think you really are something wonderful. Before long, the date arrives to report at the Missionary Training Center (often called the MTC). After the orientation there, the parents go out one door and the missionaries another, and the training begins. Somehow the suits feel foreign, the ties seem tight, the wake-up calls come too early, and the classes are intense. You study twelve to fifteen hours a day and follow a strict schedule. When fatigue has set in, one of your MTC instructors decides to teach another hour on language training. A few prospective missionaries turn in their badges and choose the easy course. Sure, it will be embarrassing to go home, they think, but the people at home just don't know what the MTC is really like.

Day after day, you are asked to go beyond what you are sure is your limit. Others may call it quits, and you may even consider quitting yourself. But you are no quitter. You set your jaw and decide you can take anything for three weeks (eight weeks if you are learning a foreign language). There are spiritual highs almost daily, and the food (although not like Mom's cooking) isn't lethal. You learn to love your companion and roommates. But about the time you start getting the hang of it, your time at the MTC is over.

The farewells at the airport are not as bad as that first day at the MTC. You are pumped, ready to go. After a plane ride, you get off the plane into the welcome arms of your new mission president and his wife. The assistants to the president (APs) look so mature and polished. You are sure you will never be able to become like them. You won't remember much of the orientation because your brain was overloaded in the MTC. You get your first assignment, and you are sure the world has just been introduced to a modern-day Ammon.

But after two or three weeks with a companion who isn't perfect, you wonder why you are there. You may be verbally attacked by a well-meaning but misdirected "Christian" who wants to save your soul. You have been praying so many times a day that you lose count. Your companion has no mercy. He only wants to talk about scriptures and doctrines. He wants you to read, memorize, pray, talk to total strangers, and use the scriptures to defend your beliefs. Finally, your companion wants you to be happy and enthusiastic all the time.

Unfortunately, some missionaries find themselves throwing up on the sidelines, unwilling to continue until they have made up for their lack of spiritual and physical preparation. Times of discouragement come, and they don't feel like talking things out. They want to be alone, but the "White Bible" (*Missionary Handbook*) says you must always be with your companion. Thankfully, nobody dies from the adjustment period of a mission. But if even one missionary drops out during the adjustment period, that is one too many.

What can you do to lessen the shock of adjustment? This book will examine what a missionary does and give you some helpful insights on how to more effectively prepare for your mission. Your mission can and will be the greatest eighteen months or two years of your life to that point if you are prepared to serve. Start preparing today by doing what missionaries do. What a shame it is to be unprepared when it's your time to play. It is a real honor to be on the Lord's varsity team during the last minutes of the fourth quarter of the greatest game ever played. The opposition is well trained and desperate. They know that when the game is over (at the second coming of the Savior), they will be locked away in darkness for a long time. Their main objective is to make everyone as miserable as possible. They do this by subtly convincing you that you can prepare when you step onto the playing field. But preparation eliminates the fear of failure, and you are not called to fail. If you are prepared, you will not fail. Your mission president will look forward to welcoming you onto the team. But how grateful he will be if you have taken your preparation seriously. Good luck as you play your designated few minutes. Prepare now to serve with honor!

Studying the Scriptures

IT IS ALWAYS A MARVEL to listen to recently returned missionaries give their homecoming talks. It may be hard for you to see yourself doing that in just a few short years. Returned missionaries seem so experienced and professional in matching various scriptures to specific doctrines and personal testimony. But how did they get that way?

If you put off learning how to study the scriptures until you are on your mission, you are sentencing yourself to some embarrassing times and some long nights. I speak from first-hand experience. On the very day our group landed in Samoa (where I served my first mission), the district leader took me to visit a minister of another religion. After some pleasant introductory remarks, he started attacking my beliefs, using my own scriptures. He knew far more about the doctrine of our church than I did. I remembered reading a scripture I might have used to answer his questions, but I had no idea where to find it. By the end of his verbal thrashing, I was totally humiliated. I sure wished I had paid more attention in Sunday School and priesthood meeting. I also wished I had listened better during seminary and youth firesides. But now it was too late.

It was probably a good thing there wasn't a plane heading back to the United States or I might have been tempted to get on it. I decided then that I would never let such a thing happen to me again. In the next three weeks, studying day and night, I completely read the Standard Works. I must admit I probably slept through part of the Old Testament. The New Testament was more familiar (except for some of Paul's writings), while the Book of Mormon was very familiar (except for the Isaiah part of 2 Nephi!). But both the Doctrine and Covenants and Pearl of Great Price were totally new to me. What had I read during my youth? If only I had studied those books before starting on my mission!

How can you motivate yourself to read the scriptures? Don't make it drudgery. Set a regular time to read every day—right when you wake up in the morning, during your lunch break, or just before you go to bed at night. Don't try reading when you are exhausted, because you'll just fall asleep. If you could discipline yourself to read for thirty minutes a day, that would be great. If you can't take that much, work up to it by starting with five or ten minutes a day. The key is to get into the habit of *daily scripture study*. If you are in seminary, take advantage of the required reading schedule. Experiment by reading aloud; it may help you retain more.

Once you have a set time each day, find your scriptures and put them where you plan to study. Avoid wasting precious study time hunting for them. If you are really serious about preparing, you might consider buying your missionary scriptures now and marking them as you read. Parents, grandparents, and others are often glad to buy scriptures for Christmas or for your birthday. Use a red pencil (or a dry marker) to highlight scriptures you want to remember. But don't get a marker that will bleed through the pages! When I marked my first set of scriptures, I used a red pen. Although it was economical, marking one verse would automatically mark a verse on the back of the page (and sometimes several more when my scriptures got a little moist from the high humidity in Samoa). A bleeding pen can make your scriptures look like a disaster, so save yourself some grief and use a colored pencil.

Don't lie on your bed to study; you sleep in bed. Your brain will automatically tell your body to go to sleep if you try reading there. Sit up in a well-lighted place. Turn off the TV and radio, because they will block you from hearing the still, small voice of the Spirit.

I wish I had realized before my mission how willing Heavenly Father is to help his children understand the meaning of the scriptures. Make sure you take time to pray for help before you begin reading. It is like the difference between reading in a dark room and one that is well lighted. If you find that your reading isn't making much sense, stop and pray again for the Lord's help.

There are many ways to read the scriptures, but we will only discuss two. If you have never read the scriptures all the way through, start now. Your testimony will be much more powerful if you can truthfully say that you have read the Book of Mormon and know that it is true. How can you testify if you have never read it or prayed about it? It is not very convincing to say, "Well, I think it is true" or "My mom told me it was true." It may be necessary to rely on the testimony of others until you get your own, but don't cheat yourself of blessings you can, with effort, have yourself.

So first, *read to understand the story*. Whose father was Mosiah? Why were the sons of Mosiah on a fourteen-year mission among the Lamanites? Did Moses live before or after Abraham? Which one of the four Gospels contains most of the parables? Why is the Book of Moses found in the Pearl of Great Price rather than in the Bible? Once you read all the way through the Standard Works, you will find it much easier to remember important facts and details of the big picture.

You are not necessarily reading for depth but for content; depth will come with time and study. The degrees of glory (D&C 76) will become a favorite. The much-talked-about Word of Wisdom (D&C 89) will not be difficult to remember. Although finding the temptations of Jesus may prove more challenging, don't be overwhelmed at the thousands of names, places, and events recorded in the scriptures. Just take it a bit at a time.

As you continue to read for the story, you may find a topic that catches your interest. Finish the story, then come back during the latter part of your study session and "posthole"—find out more about the subject that interested you. You can use the Topical Guide, the Bible Dictionary, other reference books, or whatever you like. At first, it might be challenging to know the right questions to ask. But after you've had some practice, you will find that thirty minutes isn't long enough. Then you will start to look forward to your study sessions, and you may want to study the scriptures instead of watching TV. You might want to study with some of your friends who should also be preparing for missions.

If you find words you don't understand, write them down. Then look them up or ask someone to explain them to you. Mom and Dad may actually be smarter than you think! An older brother or sister who has served a mission is a great source of answers. A seminary or institute teacher can usually help. A quorum advisor or Sunday School teacher will be glad to give the question a try. Every once in a while, you won't be able to find an answer to your question. Be patient. Just because you don't know the answer doesn't mean there isn't one. In situations like this, just put the question on hold in your mind and continue your study. Eventually you'll find the answer; when you do, you will never forget it, because you will have paid the price to learn it for yourself.

Look for promises in the scriptures. These promises are like a mathematical formula: if you do X and Y, you will get Z, a certain blessing. With time and experience, you will discover that every blessing you want from your Heavenly Father (including the ability to read and understand the scriptures!) has a formula in the scriptures. Be patient as you search for them.

As you read, ask yourself, "What question would this scripture answer?" As you begin to perfect this technique, your confidence will increase and your testimony will grow stronger—you will be prepared to answer questions. But remember, do not use your knowledge of the scriptures to attack others, because the spirit of contention is not of God. The first time I read Doctrine and Covenants 6:16, I asked myself, "What question would someone have to ask so I could use this verse as the answer?" The question was, "Can Satan read our thoughts?" The very next day an investigator asked me that question. I excitedly turned to the scripture. Both the investigator and my companion were pleasantly surprised that I could find the scripture to clear up the problem. This situation triggered a personal formula for reading the scriptures: I always ask myself, "What has the Lord said about this topic?" As a missionary, your responsibility is to show your investigators what and why (when applicable) the Lord has revealed, not to argue about doctrines.

It is an exciting challenge to use the scriptures to document every belief you have. This approach will set you apart as being well-prepared from the first day you arrive in your mission area. Use whatever strategy or gimmick you can to help you remember where important scriptures are located. It will be like learning a new language: with practice, hard work, and sacrifice, you will be able to recall the things you have studied when you need them.

The more you study the scriptures, the more exciting they become. Although scripture mastery is difficult, I think Heavenly Father made it difficult so only those who are really serious will pay the price to learn. Read the scriptures with the idea of teaching someone else. Ask yourself, "How would I explain this part to someone else?" The scriptures offer a chance to enter a new and insightful world. So open the door!

LEARNING TO TEACH

MOST OF US ENVISION A MISSION as two missionaries sitting in the homes of investigators, teaching them the missionary discussions. This certainly is a major part of a mission, so look at yourself now. How often do you get an opportunity to practice teaching? Some people have the mistaken idea that teaching is just standing in front of a class and talking. But this approach will only bring you heartache and disappointment. Teaching is one of the most difficult exercises in the world.

Most likely, your opportunities to teach may seem limited. However, with a little creative thinking, you will discover that the Lord and his church have provided many opportunities for even the young to practice their teaching skills. There are several experiences that will polish your teaching skills quickly and effectively.

Home teaching is the most often overlooked teaching opportunity. At least once a month, young men have the opportunity to teach in a situation that parallels the missionary experience more closely than any other. You and your companion visit a family to teach them the gospel of Jesus Christ. Remarkable! But what if your senior companion always teaches the lesson? Well, why don't you shock him by volunteering to teach the next one? If he is hesitant (which he won't be), remind him that you are trying to develop your teaching skills for your mission. Although it is recommended that you teach from the First Presidency message in the *Ensign,* you might ask your companion and the family if you can also teach the missionary discussions. You would be light years ahead of other missionaries if you could enter the MTC with the experience of teaching all six discussions. You would know what questions to ask your MTC instructors, and you would know your strengths and weaknesses. As you teach, you will be more motivated to learn the scriptures and doctrines as you discuss sacred things with others.

Many missionaries are shy and lack confidence in their ability to teach effectively. These skills can be strengthened a great deal with a little experience. Month after month you will see different reactions to different teaching styles. You will need to adjust your style to meet people's needs rather than expecting others to accommodate your style. Encourage them to ask questions so you will develop skills in answering. The moment of truth is when you ask them to evaluate your teaching. If they are honest, they will have some suggestions in areas where you might improve. You might find out that you have distracting habits, like scratching your nose. Being aware of such habits makes them much easier to overcome. These people love you and want you to succeed. They will be much more patient than many investigators who haven't developed those feelings of closeness. Try to change your weaknesses into strengths before you leave.

Visiting teaching gives women the same opportunity. Although the Relief Society permits making contact over the phone if other attempted visits fail, the value of face-to-face teaching far outweighs the inconvenience of repeated call-backs. It will also give you valuable practice in contacting evasive investigators.

Giving a talk in church is another great teaching experience. It has become a common practice for the youth to choose an interesting article from the *New Era* and read it to the congregation. Although this method helps polish your public reading skills, it doesn't do much for your teaching skills. Seek for opportunities to speak in church. Then take full advantage by preparing your talk from the ground up. Although the youth sometimes criticize boring talks given by adults, you will find it requires some honest work to prepare interesting talks.

How do you prepare an interesting and informative talk? First, decide on the *purpose* or *problem* of your talk by deciding what you want to accomplish. For example, you might write on a piece of paper, "The purpose of my talk is to encourage members of the Church to read their scriptures every day." Or you might state it in the form of a problem: "A problem we all face as members of the Church is regular scripture reading as a family." A specific purpose or problem will guide you in your preparation.

Next, ask yourself, "If I could say only three or four things about this topic, what would I say?" This approach usually helps you focus on a couple of ideas you feel are important for people to understand. Limit yourself to three or four main ideas. They are so important that if the speaker before you takes almost all your time, you need at least enough time to read your main ideas before you bear your testimony and sit down.

After you have identified your main ideas, look for inspirational stories, appropriate scriptures, and personal examples to expand each of the main ideas. These can be called

16

expansions because they do not stand alone but merely enlarge upon the main ideas. Make sure this information helps clarify the main ideas and is not just something to take up time. If the speakers in front of you take too much time, you can shorten your talk by eliminating or condensing the number of stories, scriptures, and examples. Never eliminate the main ideas! If a speaker doesn't show up and you have more time to take, just add some more expansion materials. Don't try to come up with a new main idea. The buffer that enables you to lengthen or shorten your talk without sacrificing the main ideas is the expansion section.

The final part of your talk is your testimony. Your testimony tells people how strongly you believe in what you have been saying. Don't wander with your testimony; focus on what you have been talking about. You may want to set up your talk using the following format:

Purpose or problem:	Scripture study
Main Ideas	Expansions: (illustrations, scriptures, examples, stories)
1.	1.
	a.
	b.
2.	2.
3.	3.
Testimony:	I believe . . .

This format will enable you to stop exactly when you are supposed to without sacrificing your talk. Those who have used this method find it easy and effective. If you have another method that works, use it. Promise yourself you will never give another boring talk.

Another opportunity to practice your teaching skills

might be as a substitute teacher in Sunday School or Primary. Let the Sunday School president know you are willing to fill in. Take your preparation seriously. The more accustomed you become to using scriptures, stories, and examples, the easier teaching the gospel becomes. Remember, the Lord commanded us to teach from the scriptures (D&C 42:12).

Yet another opportunity for teaching is at youth conferences, firesides, and discussion groups. Although you may feel afraid or anxious about teaching others, you should realize that you do have something worthwhile to say. Choose a topic relevant to the audience you are addressing. Try to get them involved by asking and answering questions and making observations. You will soon discover how difficult it is to carry the entire load yourself. When everyone is involved, teaching becomes enjoyable. Don't ever turn down an opportunity to speak, because preparation forces us to learn. Also, the challenge of teaching allows us to grow.

The final area we will discuss is where you have a captive audience to teach—during family home evening. We are commanded to meet as a family every week and teach one another the doctrine of the kingdom. It is difficult for Mom and Dad to always teach the lesson. What a pleasant surprise (more like a shock!) if you volunteer to teach regularly. If you start early enough, you will gain adequate experience in teaching almost all the gospel principles in a friendly setting before being thrust into a sometimes hostile environment. Do yourself a favor and learn how to teach.

There are many good books on the techniques of teaching. One of the best sources of insight is to keep your eyes open at school, church, or seminary. See what makes one person a good teacher and someone else marginal. When you watch (without condemning) those who are really trying, the Lord will help you learn from their mistakes as well as their successes. Even when you have a hard time concentrating in sacrament meeting, you can make a mental note of how you would teach if you were the speaker. Make a list of what makes a good speaker interesting and a boring speaker boring (to you). Practice every chance you get. The Church and the world need a lot more good teachers.

4

LEARNING TO PRAY

A MISSIONARY PRAYS A LOT because successful missionary work requires the help of the Lord. If you have learned to pray regularly, the transition to missionary life may not be that difficult. If you haven't, you may become frustrated as you try to learn in a crash course what others have learned over a lifetime.

Praying is like jogging. When you first start to get into shape, you feel like you will never make it. It is often uncomfortable, your muscles get sore, and everyone else seems faster and better. In short, you're not sure if it's worth the effort. But after the first few weeks of training, you start to get the hang of it, and jogging becomes not just doable but actually fun. The devil would have you believe it is impossible for you to communicate with God. He would have you believe only prophets and especially righteous men and women can get answers to prayer. He will whisper over and over that it isn't worth the price. But remember that Satan is "a liar from the beginning" (D&C 93:25). As with reading the scriptures, you must set some guidelines that will help you develop and fine-tune your prayers. First, decide you will pray every night and morning without fail. If you are already in the habit, this will be easy. If you are not, you will probably slip a few times before praying becomes part of your routine.

It is easier to establish the habit if you pray at a specific time every day. Rationalization will kill the development of good prayer skills.

When we were young, my brother and I used to sleep in a little shanty behind our house. As soon as it was warm enough in the spring that we wouldn't freeze, we would move from the house to the shanty, where we would stay until the first snow fell or until the nights got so cold we couldn't keep warm. It was easy to rationalize kneeling on top of the bed, because the concrete floor was so cold. Then, to maintain my concentration on prayer, it was easy to rationalize putting a blanket around my shoulders to keep out the cold. The next step seemed automatic. Why not lie down so I could be looking into heaven in case Heavenly Father wanted to give me an immediate answer? You can guess the rest of the story. Several times, I would wake up at two or three in the morning and realize I had fallen asleep in the middle of my prayer.

Pray before you are so tired you can't possibly stay awake. It may help to think of prayer as a telephone conversation with your Heavenly Father. If you called your friends and immediately started to talk, explaining how things were going and asking questions without ever giving them a chance to answer your questions or respond to your comments, they might consider you rude. Yet we often do the same thing in our prayers. As a young man, I'm afraid I often "told" the Lord how things were and instructed him how to answer my prayers. Perhaps that is why I didn't receive many recognizable answers to my prayers. The answers were there, but I wasn't "tuned in" and listening for them. In later life, I have come to know that effective prayer requires some preparation. It is helpful to get into the mood of prayer by mentally reviewing the day or the plans for the day. Make a mental list of things you want to "talk over" with Heavenly Father. Make a second list of questions, needs, or concerns you may have. If you are having trouble getting into the spirit of prayer, you might try listening to some Church music or reading a chapter from the Book of Mormon. It took me a long time to realize you can't rush a prayer. Just going through the motions doesn't do much good. A sincere and honest prayer will change your life and the lives of those around you.

Sometimes a walking prayer is effective. You don't always have to be on your knees—although that position helps keep your mind focused on what you are doing. Concentrate on your words and focus on listening for the Spirit. Then your mind will not wander nearly so often. Learn to listen more than you talk in prayer. Heavenly Father knows all the answers and is willing to answer every sincere prayer. Your main problem will not be getting an answer to prayer but learning to recognize the answer when it comes.

Someone said, "General answers come from general prayers, and specific answers come from specific prayers." Specific answers usually make a profound impression, so learn to recognize how the Lord answers your prayers. He may give you an excited, tingling sensation all over your body. He may choose to give you a sudden rush of ideas. He may give you a calm, peaceful, right feeling. His answers may move you to tears. But be careful, because although spiritual experiences are often accompanied by strong emotions, all strong emotions should not be confused with spiritual experiences. How Heavenly Father answers your prayers may be different from how he responds to prayers of your parents, brothers, sisters, or friends. It is important that you discover for yourself how to communicate with God.

Don't try to dictate to the Lord when he should answer your prayers. Some prayers take years before the answer is realized. Some will be answered before you finish praying. Many missionaries have told me they received answers to prayers anywhere from a day to a few weeks later because they were specifically watching for them. A number of the missionaries lamented at having missed answers to prayers because they failed to watch for them.

"Asking in faith" requires that you expect an answer. After nearly three and a half years of waiting for the next dramatic answer to prayer, Joseph Smith recorded, "I betook myself to prayer and supplication to Almighty God for forgiveness of all my sins and follies, and also for a manifestation to me, that I might know of my state and standing before him; *for I had full confidence in obtaining a divine manifestation,* as I previously had one" (Joseph Smith–History 1:29; emphasis added). You may be surprised at how willing Heavenly Father is to reveal answers to your questions and problems.

If the answer does not come immediately, don't be discouraged. Sometimes we aren't doing anything wrong, we just haven't done it long enough. Daniel prayed and fasted for three full weeks on a pressing problem before he finally received an answer. When the answer came, he learned that *he* was holding up the process, not God (see Daniel 10:2–12). What a lesson for us: we can receive whatever we want from our Heavenly Father as soon as we are willing to receive it. We need to let our Heavenly Father determine when we are really ready.

Avoid the "Heavenly Father, bless the food" type of

prayers. Nothing is wrong with a sincere blessing on the food. As you pray, make sure your heart and mind are really focused. Late one night, I came home from work exhausted. I went to the shanty and fell on my knees for my nightly prayer. "Heavenly Father, bless the food," I said. Oops, wrong prayer. I knew I had to do better than that, because I was wasting my time and the attention of the great Governor of the whole universe. Later, I discovered that Moroni felt the need to use his father Mormon's teachings to instruct the Nephites on the same issue: "[It is] counted evil unto a man, if he shall pray and not with real intent of heart; yea, and *it profiteth him nothing,* for God receiveth none such" (Moroni 7:9; emphasis added).

Prayer, when properly engaged in and understood, can be one of the greatest sources of comfort and insight. You can't expect to become an expert in prayer by offering a few isolated prayers any more than you can expect to become a great lecturer by giving an occasional lecture. Practice does make perfect, and perfect practice makes perfect prayer. You will never regret the time you spend praying because it will enrich your life, help you avoid temptation, and remind you of life's eternal perspective. As Alma counseled his faithful son Helaman, "Look to God and live" (Alma 37:47).

Getting Along with Others

GETTING ALONG WITH COMPANIONS and other missionaries is one of the more difficult adjustments for a missionary. But why is it so difficult? Unfortunately, too many missionaries have learned and adopted the "fight or flight" philosophy.

The "fight or flight" philosophy allows only for an extreme reaction—either fight with your companion and others or run away when problems arise. But you may argue, "Well, I'll get along with my companion and others because they are not like my brother or sister." Don't bet on it! The same principles necessary to get along with companions will help you bring peace and harmony to your family. You may think you brother is a reject from the war in heaven, so nobody expects you to get along with him. Wrong again. He is described by our Heavenly Father (who doesn't make mistakes) as one of his choice sons—a noble and great one (see Abraham 3:22–24). Your little sister may be so silly and giggly she drives you crazy. You may find the same or worse on your mission with children of members and investigators, or even some companions. You can expect to encounter all types of people.

The thing to do is learn now how to get along with people. How is it to be done? Start by deciding to take control of your reactions rather than letting someone else dictate how you react. Just because your little brother does something to annoy you doesn't mean you have to hit him. Fighting will never solve a problem; it will always make it worse. There are often power struggles in a family—trying to control each other's actions—and our responses are based on those situations. For example, let's say your little brother has a real mouth. He says things he knows will irritate you just so you will yell at him or hit him. He seems to enjoy the abusive attention. But you decide to take control of the situation. He mouths off in a manner that normally sets the cycle in motion. You choose not to respond. He wonders if you didn't hear, so he tries again. You smile understandingly but do not react. He wants to know if you are feeling okay. You assure him you are fine but tell him you are preparing for a mission by learning how to get along with him. He makes some statement about being sick to his stomach from your wonderful righteousness. Again you choose not to respond. As you stick to your decision, you find he starts to back off because it isn't fun to fight with yourself.

With this victory comes a sense of accomplishment and well-being. This good feeling is the Spirit bearing testimony that you are heading in the right direction. It almost becomes a game as you continue to identify and overcome the things that made you so grouchy before.

"Flight" is no more difficult to cure than "fight." For example, something goes wrong or someone does something that ticks you off. Normally you storm out of the house, slam the door, and rush to the car. With the screeching of rubber, you back out of the driveway, making sure everyone knows you are upset. You leave two parallel stripes of smoking rubber as you recklessly flee the scene. If you do this, you are watching too much television! Even though the world may solve problems by theatrically leaving the scene of confrontation, it is not acceptable for a missionary.

There will be times on your mission when you just want to get away from a stressful situation. That is all right as long as you take your companion with you! If he or she is the problem, you'd better have a "Plan B." Leaving your companion, whether you are angry or not, is dangerous, against mission rules, and could jeopardize your mission. If you have never learned to face problems without fight or flight, now is a good time to learn.

You will always have an authority figure standing over you in the mission—your trainer, your senior companion, the district leader, the zone leader, the assistants to the president, or the president himself. How can you learn to get along if you haven't practiced the skills? Start right now. When someone says something that makes you angry, learn to control your reaction. Get a hold of yourself, separate the issue from the person, and then deal only with the issue. It sounds pretty easy because it is! Say a quick prayer for help *before* you respond, and you will find you are more in control than if you speak first and think later. Some people suggest counting to ten before you say anything. If you remind yourself you love the person but disagree with what the person says, you will begin to direct your anger toward the issue and away from the person.

Set some guidelines for solving problems. Explain how the irritating comment made you feel: "When you accused me of driving recklessly, that really made me mad." You are focusing on your reaction and the cause. If you feel out of control, suggest a "cooling off" period. After you're in control, sit down and reason with the person. Learn how to talk face to face without yelling or accusing. Stay focused on the issue.

Too many teenagers try to bully or intimidate their parents by threatening to "run away" or demonstrating an "I'll show you" attitude. This is a "lose-lose" situation. Your position as a son or daughter is weakened because of the power struggle—you lose. Your parents begin to question their effectiveness as parents and wonder if it is all worth it—they lose. Try to create a "win-win" situation. If you can calmly and rationally express how you feel in a way that demonstrates to your parents you are maturing and can be trusted with the car—you win. Your parents realize that maybe they jumped to conclusions and didn't give you a fair chance to explain your side of the story, so they soften their feelings and response toward you—they win.

Rationally discussing an emotional issue does not mean you don't use forceful language to express yourself. As a missionary, you will find you disagree with your companion and investigators many times. But when you master the art of discussing without arguing, you will promote great learning experiences with a lot less stress.

As teenagers, we often feel it is our right to say what is on our mind. As an adult, you will discover that silence is sometimes the best answer to an explosive situation. In studying the life of the Savior, you will discover that he often chose to remain silent rather than argue. Learning how to be silent without sulking, pouting, or being indifferent is not easy. Watch people carefully when you react to a situation. If your silence angers them even more, maybe you need to learn to give a quiet, nonconfrontational response. When your response creates a different effect than what you wanted, figure out why it backfired and how you could have responded differently. You can generally find out what happened by asking the person to honestly tell you how he or she felt and how he or she would have liked you to respond. You can learn to "live together in love" (D&C 42:45). Every "battle" in which you control yourself is one giant victory for you on your mission.

BEING WORTHY TO SERVE

AT THE CALL OF A PROPHET, "every worthy young man" should serve a mission. Realizing that the world in which you are growing up is very challenging, President Benson counseled that "every young man should make himself worthy!" One of Satan's most deceptive tactics is to make you think you can live however you want during your teen years and still serve a mission. That is totally false.

On March 4, 1993, the First Presidency and Quorum of the Twelve Apostles issued a letter outlining the requirements for serving a mission. They also made a sobering list of those who would not be invited to serve. Unfortunately, many young people do not believe that worldly living should eliminate them from Christlike service. Realistically, you do not set the criteria for worthiness to serve.

Without reviewing the March 4, 1993, letter (your priesthood leaders should do that with you!), let us focus on some broad areas of worthiness you need to know about and on how to repent if necessary. You might wonder why the Lord and his leaders make such an issue out of worthiness. First, it is impossible to pull people onto higher ground if you are not standing there yourself. To preach one thing and live another is called hypocrisy, and no one wants to learn from a hypocrite.

Second, the Lord requires such a high standard of obedience because when you hold up the light to lead others to Christ, it automatically illuminates every chink in your own armor. The devil will take full advantage of this and make you feel unworthy to serve. Unless you have successfully taken care of the problems of the past, you will suffer beyond anything you have suffered to this point.

The third reason the Lord is anxious for you to be worthy is that he has many lessons to teach you while you serve your mission. Although personal improvement is not the main reason for your going on a mission, it is one of the blessings that come from worthy service. If you are not worthy, your sins make it impossible for the Spirit to teach you everything the Lord has in mind for you to learn.

What are the major areas of unworthiness that need to be corrected before your mission? The first mention is morality. You may be saying, "Oh no, another lecture on staying morally clean!" If it were not of paramount importance, the Lord and his leaders would not mention it so frequently. Alma the Younger taught his wayward missionary son Corianton the seriousness of moral sins: "Know ye not, my son, that these [sexual sins] are an abomination in the sight of the Lord; yea, most abominable above all sins save it be the shedding of innocent blood or denying the Holy Ghost?" (Alma 39:5). Satan knows he can't tempt many people to murder. Because of your lack of experience, it is impossible for you to "deny the Holy Ghost." The next most serious sin that can disqualify you from fulfilling your foreordained mission is immorality.

There are more shades of immorality than there are shades of green, ranging all the way from self-abuse (masturbation) to fornication and adultery. These serious acts include necking and petting, watching pornographic movies, looking at filthy magazines, exhibitionism, voyeurism (being a "Peeping Tom"), and homosexual behavior. Why are they all so serious? Because they tempt you to abuse or pervert the power to give life. If our goal is to become like the Father of Life, then we must be tested in the areas that deal with the sanctity of life. If we continually abuse the powers of life during our mortal existence, then naturally those powers will be taken from us in the life to come. If a pre-med student failed every undergraduate course in physiology, chemistry, and biology, you would not be surprised if he or she were refused admittance into medical school and therefore never became a doctor. So it is with becoming like our Heavenly Father. Unless we learn to master the things that make him like he is, we can't expect to be given the opportunity to become like him.

If you have problems in the area of morality, the Lord requires you to see your bishop immediately. You may say, "Oh, that would be too embarrassing!" Embarrassing or not, that is what the Lord requires. In Doctrine and Covenants 58:42–43, the Lord gives us the formula we must follow if we are to receive a forgiveness of our sins: "Behold, he who repenteth of his sins, the same is forgiven, and I, the Lord, remember them no more. By this ye may know if a man repenteth of his sins—behold, he will confess them and forsake them." You and I can't dictate to the Lord what we will do to gain forgiveness. He has revealed a two-part process: Forsaking (not doing it again, either physically or mentally) is only half of the formula; we must also confess to the proper authority.

Won't the bishop think less of you when you tell him what you have done? Just the opposite. He realizes how difficult it is and how much courage it takes to confess. His respect for you will only increase. Won't he remember what you have done every time he sees you after you confess? Absolutely not. As a mission president, I relearned one of the great lessons about forgiveness. When missionaries came to clear past transgressions that had come back to haunt them, I would listen to the confession, counsel with them, and conclude with prayer. A month or two later, some would say, "President, do you remember what we talked about last time?" I honestly could not remember. I started to worry that I was losing my mind. Then a real insight came. Since I represented the Lord in taking the confession, after it had been forsaken and confessed and the Lord remembered it no more, there was no reason for me to continue to remember it. What a revelation!

When you go to see the bishop, you will feel as if a weight is on your shoulders. After you have confessed, you will feel that the weight has been lifted and you are free and light for the first time since the transgression. You will wonder why you waited so long to clear up the past. Will the bishop ever tell anyone about your sins? Absolutely not! He is bound by the strictest vow of confidentiality. Even if he is threatened by the law, he is duty bound not to tell anyone. Seldom, if ever, does a bishop break that confidence. In spite of the stories you may have heard, it is usually the transgressor or partner in sin, not the bishop, who spreads the story.

What is so bad about watching a few R-rated movies or looking at bad magazines? No one may have told you about the devastating feelings of guilt and worthlessness you feel when you are standing in the waters of baptism or laying your hands on a sick person's head and a "flashback" from a movie or magazine centerfold appears before your eyes. In the very minute when you want the Spirit more than anything else, Satan brings back your past behavior to plague you. I have tried to comfort weeping elders who wanted to know if they would ever be able to rid themselves of the bad thoughts and vivid pictures they participated in before they became serious about life. I genuinely hurt with them, but all I could say was that the Lord in his own time would help them erase the memories.

President David O. McKay gave us this counsel: "Tell me what you think about when you do not have to think, and I will tell you what you are. Temptation does not come to those who have not thought of it before. Keep your thoughts clean, and it will be easy to resist temptations as they come" (*Gospel Ideals* [Salt Lake City: Deseret News Press, 1953], p. 401). You are fooling yourself to believe you can watch pornography and, with a wave of the hand, erase those images from your mind. The price you will pay will be far greater than the money you spent buying those materials. Do yourself a favor and avoid like a plague any movie, magazine, video, or song that causes your mind to take a low, dirty trail.

If you are struggling to control self-abuse, seek the help of your bishop. That may sound silly, but you may need someone with priesthood authority to help you get control. Perhaps a related story will give you some ideas on how to use your bishop's help. Just after my wife and I were engaged, an alert bishop called us in to warn us about the increased temptations we would face before our planned temple marriage. He said, "I want you two to promise me that before you become involved with each other physically, you will call and ask for my permission!" I looked at Sister Bott and she looked at me, and we started to laugh. How ridiculous—ask the bishop if we can be immoral! But he continued, "That is exactly what I want you to do. You see, when you get into a cycle of increased intimacy, it is really easy to go too far before you realize you are out of control. If you will promise to call me, that will break the cycle, and you'll be able to regain control." We promised and went on our way. Some weeks later, we were sitting admiring the lights of the Logan Temple and planning our life after marriage. Absolutely nothing was happening. My fiancée looked up at me and asked, "Do you think we ought to call the bishop?" We both started to laugh. I took my arm from around her, took her for a soft drink, and then took her home. It may have been silly, but we made it to the temple worthily.

I used to tell the missionaries who were struggling with personal problems to call me anytime, day or night. Only twice in three years did I receive a phone call—once at 12:30 A.M. and once at 2:00 A.M. We talked about their favorite subject, about how the work was going, and about the next zone conference. After about ten or fifteen minutes, they would suggest that I might be tired. My response was, "Not unless you are." They would thank me for my time and hang up. Silly? Probably, but they made it through the time of temptation without falling. Your bishop would also be more than willing to receive some late-night phone calls if that is what it takes. More often than not, you will have the phone in your hand and say to yourself, "I can control this. I don't need to call the bishop. Get thee hence, Satan." And you will be okay. Use whatever defenses you need to break undesirable habits.

When you are tempted, use the temptation as a catalyst to remind you to read a chapter out of the Book of Mormon, memorize a scripture, say a prayer, sing a song, memorize a poem, or do whatever is reasonably necessary to help you make it through the temptation. You will never be in a situation you can't control unless you exercise your agency against the counsel of your leaders.

If you have trouble with swearing, now is the time to overcome it. I have been embarrassed for missionaries who obviously had never learned how to express themselves in an acceptable way without swearing. At the most inappropriate times, they would cut loose with a curse. Dead silence would follow, with all eyes focused on them. They were embarrassed, and we hurt for them. It is far better to learn to say exactly what you mean and how you feel without using inappropriate language. Think before you speak and increase your vocabulary so you do not need to swear.

If you have developed the habit of lying to avoid the consequences of your bad choices, get in the habit of being totally truthful. A lie only compounds the transgression. If you make a conscious effort to tell the truth, you will find it isn't very long until lying becomes so offensive you can't believe you ever did it. For example, if you are pulled over by a policeman for speeding, watch his startled reaction as you admit you were in error and express a willingness to pay the penalty. Don't try to lie your way out of it. We all have some changing to do.

If you are troubled with the habit of taking things that don't belong to you, learn how to control the urge now. You have been born into a "something for nothing" generation. As a representative of the Lord, you need to adjust your thinking to reflect the teachings of the Church: "There is a law irrevocably decreed in heaven before the foundation of this world, upon which all blessings are predicated—and when we obtain any blessing from God, it is by obedience to that law upon which it is predicated" (D&C 130:20–21). There really is no free lunch. How sad to see the trust destroyed between companions when one "borrows" something that belongs to the other without asking. Face the problem if you have it; you can overcome the tendency with an attitude change.

If you have a filthy mind—always seeing something dirty in everything that is said—start today to eliminate those thoughts. No one likes to be around a filthy-minded person. You cannot engage in telling or listening to dirty jokes or stories and expect that your mind will not become tainted. Refuse to engage in conversations that make light of sacred things. The power to procreate is a sacred power. Just look at what the world calls "funny," and you will have a pretty good idea of the areas to avoid. Most of what is seen as "comedy" on television and in the movies is nothing but filth. You will find that your preparation for a mission is greatly accelerated when you turn off the television and open the scriptures and other good books.

There may be many other areas in which you need to take an aggressive role in making yourself worthy. Decide what you need to be like as a missionary, then determine where you are now and start to change. The fact that your problem has not been mentioned here does not excuse you from correcting it so you can be worthy to serve.

BEING PHYSICALLY PREPARED

SERVING A MISSION IS ONE of the most physically demanding things you will ever do. You wouldn't think going out and teaching people would be that strenuous. What makes a mission so physically demanding?

Every mission follows a regular schedule: up at 6:30 A.M., prepare to proselyte from 7:00 until 9:30 A.M., proselyte until 9:30 P.M., study until 10:30 P.M., then go to bed. On the surface, it sounds easy. But let's look a little closer.

Up to this time in your life, there has probably always been someone else to prepare good nutritious meals. Now you must do most of the cooking yourself. Energy to keep you going during the day is obtained from the food you eat. If you haven't learned how to plan, prepare, and cook good meals, you may be tempted just to eat whatever is convenient. Nutrition from junk food, although an immediate source of energy, is short-lived. Before long, your body cries out for something more stable.

From the moment the thought enters your mind (maybe as you read this book), you should start collecting nutritious menus and shopping lists for different meals. Store them in a booklet or file folder. Practice cooking each one until you are proficient at preparing the meal. Your companions will love you forever.

Start evaluating your diet now. If you are a "junk food junky," start replacing junk foods with good foods. Your ability to maintain your health will determine, to a large degree, the success you enjoy as a missionary. If either you or your companion is constantly sick, you will greatly multiply the problems in keeping the Spirit. When the messengers go down, the message doesn't get delivered.

If an evaluation of your physical condition reveals that you are carrying too much weight, get on a sensible diet and exercise program. If you are excessively overweight or have serious health problems, you may not be permitted to serve a full-time mission.

In many places, missionaries either walk or ride bicycles. If you are out of shape, it will be a real shock to your system the first time your companion wants to bike thirty miles to a teaching appointment. I remember walking ten miles between villages in Samoa in the blistering heat and stifling humidity. I thought I had died and gone to the wrong place.

You can do yourself a real favor by getting on a cycling, jogging, or hiking program. If you are out of shape when you arrive and you exert yourself, you will tend to go to sleep when you stop walking or biking. It is really poor etiquette when you can't stay awake during a discussion because you are physically exhausted.

Teaching is fatiguing. The sheer mental exertion of trying to help someone understand important gospel concepts is tiring. Teaching several discussions a day will take its toll, and you will come home at night physically exhausted. I don't know of any effective way to overcome teaching fatigue. But I do know that if you are physically out of shape to begin with, teaching becomes an almost impossible strain.

A healthy body is able to fight strange diseases much

easier than a sickly body. Also, when you are ill, your mind isn't as alert as when you are well. Feeling "under the weather" all the time makes learning a real chore. If you are constantly sick, you soon become discouraged and are tempted to give up. Before you go on your mission, you are required to get a number of shots. They are for your protection, but they also signal some of the unusual diseases you may encounter. Stay as healthy as you can as you prepare to serve.

Many places in the world have foods that are strange and exotic. Some foods you have heard of but were sure you would never eat. When your love for the people grows and your desire not to offend them surpasses your resolve not to eat their food, you may end up eating some strange things. If you are a picky eater at home, you will give yourself a lot of stress during your mission. Practice eating at least a little of everything served to you. Some of the most stressful problems between companions have come when one of them has made a big issue about not wanting to eat some of the native food.

If your body is healthy, your system can process unfamiliar foods without becoming ill. If you are teetering on the brink of being sick already, a little strange food can push you over the edge. On rare occasions, the food you are served may be tainted or spoiled. Then you will need all the strength you can muster to preserve your health. Of course, you wouldn't knowingly eat anything that would make you sick, but you may find out too late that the food was not good.

On their preparation days, missionaries often like to get together and play games. If you are grossly out of shape, it makes you the odd man out. Even though you may not be a great sports enthusiast, you will want to participate in some athletic events just so your companion won't miss out. Missionaries who are out of shape get injured more easily than those in good physical condition. Crutches make it tough to get from place to place. Many missions have banned competitive basketball because of the number of work-hindering injuries.

Occasionally, the schedule you keep as a missionary may get messed up. A few late-night blessings, a night or two taking care of your sick companion, a few nights of arbitrating problems between missionaries in your zone or district—all put a strain on your physical health. Those who plan for such stresses and are in good physical condition are able to handle the problems without getting sick themselves. Those barely making it during the best of times often find themselves seeking medical help to keep going.

Extreme weight loss or gain during a mission puts a strain on more than just your wardrobe. If you are physically active before entering the MTC, you will find weight control is much easier. It is expensive to buy several new suits or dresses after you have been on a mission three or four months. The overall message is, to be wise, get in shape now so you don't have to spend the rest of your mission wishing you had.

RECOGNIZING THE SPIRIT

ONE OF THE STATEMENTS THAT shocked me the most as a mission president was an elder or sister saying, "President, I don't think I've ever had a spiritual experience." How could that be? They were full-time missionaries whose responsibility was to help people recognize the Spirit so they would make the commitment to join the Church. As we worked with the missionaries, we began to realize that all of them had experienced many spiritual experiences, but some missionaries did not know how to recognize them.

What does the Spirit feel like? Maybe a better question is, "What do I feel like when the Spirit is with me?" If you asked a dozen missionaries how they know when the Spirit is present, you would probably get twelve different answers. One might say, "Well, I feel tingly all over." Another might describe the feeling as "total peace and serenity." Yet another might say, "My mind gets going a million miles an hour." Still another might describe the experience as exciting and activating. Each one would describe individual reactions to the Spirit. Also, different situations may trigger different responses to the Spirit.

Let's look at how several prophets have described the Spirit. Moroni was so impressed with his father's way of explaining spiritual things that he quoted Mormon as follows: "All things which are good cometh of God; and that which is evil cometh of the devil; for the devil is an enemy unto God, and fighteth against him continually, and inviteth and enticeth to sin, and to do that which is evil continually. But behold, that which is of God inviteth and enticeth to do good continually; wherefore, every thing which inviteth and enticeth to do good, and to love God, and to serve him, is *inspired* of God (Moroni 7:12–13; emphasis added).

You have been inspired of God if you have ever been prompted to do good, have felt feelings of gratitude and love toward God, or have been motivated to serve God (such as going on a mission!). In other words, you have had a spiritual experience. Think about the times you have stopped to help a child who has fallen off a bicycle. Think about the times you have decided to wash the dishes, clean the house, or mow the lawn for your mom or dad. You have been inspired by the Spirit. Think of the times you have thanked your Heavenly Father in prayer (private or public) for the Church or the prophet or your family or your health. You have had a spiritual experience. Think of the many times you have offered a silent prayer either of thanksgiving or of asking for something. Nephi said, "If ye would hearken unto the Spirit which teacheth a man to pray ye would know that ye must pray; for the evil spirit teacheth not a man to pray, but teacheth him that he must not pray" (2 Nephi 32:8).

Sometimes we think we must see an angel, hear a voice, or see a vision to have a spiritual experience. While all of those things would indeed be spiritual experiences, they are only a fraction of what your Heavenly Father has defined as spiritual experiences. Perhaps the Lord's advice to Hyrum Smith is a valuable guide for us too:

Put your trust in that Spirit which leadeth to do

good—yea, to do justly, to walk humbly, to judge righteously; and this is my Spirit.

Verily, verily, I say unto you, I will impart unto you of my Spirit, which shall enlighten your mind, which shall fill your soul with joy; and then shall ye know, or by this shall you know, all things whatsoever you desire of me, which are pertaining unto things of righteousness, in faith believing in me that you shall receive. (D&C 11:12–14)

Let's highlight the effects the Spirit will have. It will (1) lead you to do good, (2) motivate you to be fair (just), (3) keep you from becoming proud (walk humbly), (4) help you make correct decisions (judge righteously), (5) help you think clearly and give you ideas (enlighten your mind), (6) cause you to have happy feelings (fill your soul with joy), and (7) help you learn any righteous subject you are studying. Not a bad list of benefits. I'll bet most, if not all, of those things have happened to you. It really isn't "having a spiritual experience" as much as it is "recognizing a spiritual experience" that we need.

As you prepare for your mission, take advantage of every opportunity to recognize how you feel when the Spirit is with you. As you read from the Book of Mormon and the other scriptures, pay particular attention to how you feel mentally and physically. Pay more attention to the feelings you have when you are praying. When you partake of the sacrament, note how you feel. When you bear your testimony or give a talk, notice the different feelings. Some people get "scared" just before they bear their testimony. Maybe it isn't fear at all but the Spirit preparing them to share their thoughts and feelings.

After that, if you still have difficulty recognizing the

Spirit, talk to your parents, your priesthood leader, or your Young Women adviser. Seek out someone who has had more experience. You will have a powerful affect on investigators when you can confidently declare, "Brother Brown, what you are feeling right now is the Holy Ghost bearing testimony to the truthfulness of what we have been teaching!" Put yourself in situations where you are fairly sure the Spirit is present. Grow into the principle of revelation, and you will bless your life and the lives of your investigators forever.

Developing Your Testimony

M ANY TIMES ON YOUR MISSION, your testimony will come under attack. People who think they are doing God a favor will try to "teach you a thing or two." Anti-Mormon literature will (depending on where you serve) meet you at every turn. Usually such challenges to your testimony will be easily met. Occasionally, however, the nature of a question may cause you some concern. That will especially be true if you haven't taken time to strengthen your testimony.

How do you strengthen your testimony? It really isn't difficult. The Savior taught, "If any man will do his will, he shall know of the doctrine, whether it be of God, or whether I speak of myself" (John 7:17). The easiest way to get a testimony is to live the principle about which you would like to know. There is a recognizable emptiness when a missionary bears testimony about tithing when he or she has never paid tithing. A person who has never lived the Word of Wisdom does not enjoy the same advantage as one who has been tempted but resisted. The missionary who testifies that the Book of Mormon is true without having read it lacks the converting power that brings investigators into the Church. So with every principle of the gospel—live it and then testify of it.

Elder Boyd K. Packer gave a marvelous talk entitled,

"The Candle of the Lord" in which he said, "Oh, if I could teach you this one principle! A testimony is to be found in the bearing of it." How do you get the rock-solid testimony about the Savior, the Church, the prophet, or the plan of salvation? It is difficult to "live" those. But Elder Packer teaches true doctrine: "Stand up in fast and testimony meeting and bear your testimony about that which you feel you know something but are not totally sure. In the very process of your testifying, the Holy Ghost will bear unmistakable testimony to you that what you are saying is true." The Lord confirms this method of gaining a testimony when he says,

> Lift up your voices unto this people; speak the thoughts that I *shall* [note the future tense] put into your hearts, and you shall not be confounded before men; for it *shall* [again, note the future tense] be given you in the very hour, yea, in the very moment, what ye shall say. But a commandment I give unto you, that ye shall declare whatsoever thing ye declare in my name, in solemnity of heart, in the spirit of meekness, in all things. And I give unto you this promise, that inasmuch as ye do this the Holy Ghost shall be shed forth in bearing record unto all things whatsoever ye shall say. (D&C 100:5–8; emphasis added by Elder Packer)

Moroni 10:3–5 is a famous scripture often learned in seminary and Sunday School. It tells us how to gain a testimony of the Book of Mormon. Let's consider the entire formula for gaining a testimony:

> Behold, I would exhort you that when ye shall *read* these things, if it be wisdom in God that ye should read them, that ye would *remember* how merciful the Lord

hath been unto the children of men, from the creation of Adam even down until the time that ye shall *receive* these things, and *ponder* it in your hearts.

And when ye shall *receive* these things, I would exhort you that ye would *ask* God, the Eternal Father, in the name of Christ, if these things are not true; and if ye shall *ask* with a *sincere heart,* with *real intent,* having *faith in Christ,* he will manifest the truth of it unto you, by the power of the Holy Ghost. And by the power of the Holy Ghost ye may know the truth of all things. (Moroni 10:3–5; emphasis added)

Often we think that if we just "read" and "ask," the answer will be given. Too often, we suffer disappointment and frustration because the desired testimony is not obtained. No one would expect to come up with the right answer to a complex mathematical problem unless the entire formula were used. So it is with a testimony. It really does work well when we use the entire formula.

The more experiences you can have in every area relating to the Church, the easier it will be to bear your testimony. Take advantage of every opportunity to be involved. Be willing to bear your testimony frequently. You will discover certain ways of testifying that appeal to you and that will have the greatest impact on people to whom you testify. Learn to be humble, bold, and straightforward but not overbearing.

Review chapter 3 to see how many different opportunities the Lord has given you to bear your testimony. Look at the blessing the Lord promises to those who will take the challenge to bear their testimony: "Ye are blessed, for the testimony which ye have borne is recorded in heaven for the angels to look upon; and they rejoice over you, and your sins are forgiven you" (D&C 62:3). Fortunate is the mission that receives missionaries who are experienced in bearing testimony to the truthfulness of every aspect of the gospel.

BEING A SELF-STARTER

MISSIONARIES HAVE TO BE self-starters. No one is going to give you a "wake-up call" every morning. The district leader won't have time to call you every day to see if you are out of the apartment at the designated hour. The mission president can't be expected to call you every day to see if you've taken your vitamins or brushed your teeth or put on a clean pair of socks. Those are things you must learn to do on your own.

If you are in the habit of doing things for yourself without being asked or "commanded," your mission will become fun and fairly easy. If you have to be prodded to do the normal tasks you are assigned, you may be in trouble. Think about how you are doing right now. How many times do you have to be asked to take out the garbage? More than once? The Lord gave a stern warning to those who need to be reminded all the time to do what they have promised:

> It is not meet [necessary or desirable] that I should command in all things; for he that is compelled [forced] in all things, the same is a slothful and not a wise servant; wherefore he receiveth *no reward*. Verily I say, men [you and I] should be anxiously engaged in a good cause, and do many things of their own free will, and bring to pass much righteousness; for the power is

in them wherein they are agents unto themselves. And inasmuch as men do good they shall in nowise lose their reward. But he that doeth not anything *until* he is commanded, and receiveth a commandment with a doubtful heart [a bad attitude], and keepeth it with slothfulness [the least you can get away with], the same is damned [stopped in spiritual progression]. (D&C 58:26–29; emphasis added)

No reward, damned, slothful—these are hardly words to describe a faithful missionary or a person who is going to the celestial kingdom. Do yourself a big favor and start looking for ways to show your initiative. Take out the garbage before anyone has to remind you. Volunteer to scrub the toilets—it might shock your parents to death if you don't usually do things like that. Look for ways to be "anxiously engaged in a good cause." Missionaries who know how to work and are not afraid to evaluate the situation and just "do it" are loved by everyone in the mission.

Sometimes we fall into a rather childish habit of wanting people to tell us what to do. We have grown up in a world that says, "Nothing is bad unless we get caught—so what can we get away with?" Missionaries who foster this attitude before their missions are a real pain to the mission leadership until they go through an attitude adjustment.

It is no compliment when others have to tell you how to act, what to wear, or whether your hair needs to be cut. One of the signs that you are becoming an adult is your ability to recognize areas that need improvement and then (without being hounded) make whatever corrections are necessary. Maybe you need a little conscience sitting on your shoulder who whispers constantly in your ear, "The control is better when it comes from within!"

Ask yourself a couple of questions: "How do I act when I think no one is watching?" "Would I do (or say) the things I do if Mom or Dad or the bishop were here?" If the answer is less than you know you are capable of, then isn't now a good time to make the change?

Sometimes we get stuck in awkward situations. Our friends want us to do things we know are not right. Not wanting to be known as a "goody-goody," we often go along. One of the most desirable Christlike attributes is to stand for what you know is right in spite of opposition. Once you have established your reputation for not being able to be per-suaded to do wrong, your friends will start to protect you. You will also be pleasantly surprised to find that many of them will join you.

I witnessed an act of true heroism the summer before my mission. I was working for the U.S. Forest Service in a remote town in northern Idaho. There were only a couple of LDS boys in the group of fifty in the camp. During the course of the summer, the non-LDS guys tried to get us to drink and party with them. We stood our ground and refused. At the end of the summer, my friend was promoted to a position usually reserved for guys who had worked at the camp for three or four years. We were all pleased for him. The camp boss threw a party for him. At a time when everyone was at the height of the festivities, the camp boss proposed a toast to my friend. Everyone had a glass of some alcoholic drink. The boss put a glass in my friend's hand and said something like, "Just one little drink won't hurt you a bit. Just to show you really are part of the group, drink up!" The room went silent. Every eye was on him. He didn't hesitate a second, responding, "How could I be loyal to you guys if I was a trai-tor to myself and my Heavenly Father? If you really value my friendship, you won't ask me to choose between you and God!" With that declaration, he poured the drink back into the punch bowl. A huge cheer went up from everyone, including the boss. During the rest of the evening, everyone there slapped my friend on the back and expressed their appreciation for his holding his ground. They all said they knew he wouldn't give in to the pressure. I was (and still am) proud to be numbered among his friends.

Don't wait until somebody chastens you for acting or talking inappropriately. Such things can greatly injure the reputation of the Church, the mission, your family, and yourself. What a thrill it is to watch young men and women live the way they know is right in spite of the fact that no one is looking over their shoulders!

As a mission president, I always felt a lump in my throat when I would drive, unannounced, through a town far from the mission headquarters and see the missionaries peddling their bikes on the way to an appointment. On the other hand, I was always disappointed when I would visit some missionaries during the middle of the day, after 6:30 A.M., or after 9:30 P.M. and find them not doing what they had committed to do. I have listened to the most creative excuses in the world, but they are just that—*excuses.* An excuse is a weak attempt to justify unacceptable behavior. Wouldn't it be nice to be able to stand before the Savior and not worry about whether he would accept our excuses. When he asks me if I served a mission, I will respond, "I did!" When he asks if I served with honor, I will tell him I really tried. I would encourage you to live so that excuses are not necessary.

The last days (in which you now live) will require men and women who are self-starters. There is already a high demand for men and women who know how to assess the task, martial the resources, and get the job done. There will always be a place of honor for those who exercise self-control rather than waiting for someone else to impose control from outside. Number yourself among the truly noble—control yourself!

BEING AN EXAMPLE

ENVISION what a missionary looks like. In a few months (or years) you will be that vision in the mind of other young people. For too long, young people have believed they could live whatever lifestyle is comfortable during their teenage years, change just before their mission, and everything would be all right. Unfortunately, many have discovered that habits are hard to break. Let's work from the outside inward.

When you receive your mission call, it will contain a picture of what a "missionary haircut" looks like for elders. The closer your haircut resembles the model, the easier it will be to live that mission rule. Missions are stressful enough without adding additional, unnecessary stress to your life. You may think the kids at your high school will make fun of you. If you learn to use humor in tense situations now, it will benefit you when teenagers may taunt you during your mission. When an elder stands to give his farewell address and has lines clearly marking where his old hairline used to be, it is no compliment to him.

Don't try to fool yourself. Although hair length may not be a big deal to you, it is still a major issue in whether people will open their homes to you. If wearing your hair in a long hairstyle is really important to you now, it will be a constant temptation during your mission to see how close to the limit you can get without someone reminding you to get a more conservative haircut. You don't have to stand out in the crowd to be outstanding.

It is no compliment when someone has to remind you how to look. The clothes you wear as a missionary will be entirely different from your current day-to-day wardrobe. Again, if you lean toward extremes in style, you will find it difficult to wear the conservative clothes required of missionaries. I remember how difficult it was to adjust to wearing a tie all day. Before my mission, I would put the tie on just before the start of a meeting and take it off before the "amen" of the closing prayer hit the ceiling. What a shock to the system to wear a tie from before sunrise until long after dark every day of the week. You might lessen the shock by wearing a tie all day on Sunday.

Shoes talk! Without saying a word, your shoes send a powerful message about you. If you are not accustomed to polishing your shoes and keeping them clean, now is a good time to start. That doesn't mean you have to keep them spit-shined, as in the military. But scruffy shoes tell others, "I really don't care that much about myself." A good suggestion for a Christmas gift or birthday present might be a shoe-shine kit in a compact bag.

Ironing shirts does not have to be unpleasant. Spend time with your mother and have her teach you how to press suit pants and shirts. A wrinkled shirt can distract investigators so they can't concentrate on the message. Learning how to launder and iron clothes will help cut down the expense of having to replace them because they have worn out before their time.

In many parts of the world, the temperature is high and the humidity even higher. Learn to shower and use deodorants properly. Body odor turns people off. You will need to use every trick you know to keep yourself presentable if you are in a bike area or in a mission where water for showering is scarce. I remember many times bathing in the ocean and then being allowed one cup of fresh water to wash off the salty film. Rinsing with just a cup of water could be done, but it wasn't easy.

Oral hygiene is also important. Take good care of your teeth. Learn to brush and floss regularly. It is always embarrassing when a missionary needs to be told to brush his or her teeth more often and use mouthwash. Breath mints help. Avoid chewing gum as a breath freshener. Gum, unless discretely chewed, is distracting. It is better to learn before your mission to avoid bad breath by properly caring for your teeth.

You may have developed an appreciation for a wide variety of music. The music you will listen to on your mission will be limited. Too many young people go on a mission with an addiction to certain kinds of music. Some go through "withdrawal" as they are required to put that music behind them. Do yourself a favor and evaluate now the music in your listening library. Learn to listen to and appreciate Church, classical, and instrumental (not rock) music. This will help you in exchanging your present music for mission music. Don't go on a mission with the idea of rewriting the rules for appropriate music. There is purpose behind those mission rules.

Watching television is usually a forbidden activity for missionaries. Not much on TV leads you to think about God, truth, virtue, or living a Christlike life. You can't take worldly things into your mind without their having a negative effect. When a large portion of your free time is devoted to watching television, you will be tempted to do the same thing on your mission. You will be less frustrated if you have learned to go without television. Instead, read a good book (the scriptures), exercise, help around the house, or write a letter. As a missionary, you will read more than you have ever read in your whole life. If you are not accustomed to reading, your natural reaction will be to fall asleep. You can't learn much while you are sleeping; inspired dreams usually follow intense study!

Check your attitude toward other people. If you are not being helpful, kind, and considerate, you are not preparing for your mission. Being kind to those who dislike you requires more than just showing up for appointments and meetings. You must learn how to control your actions and not allow others to negatively provoke you. The Apostle Paul counseled Timothy, "Let no man despise thy youth; but be thou an example of the believers, in word, in conversation, in charity, in spirit, in faith, in purity" (1 Timothy 4:12).

How many times have you heard the age-old (but true) adage, "What you are sounds so loud in my ears that I can't hear what you are saying." Start now to eliminate any mixed messages. Make the way you act confirm what you say. Perhaps an appropriate summary of this chapter's teachings would be: "If the way you look or act draws attention to yourself and away from your message, you are dressing or acting inappropriately." Remember, you represent more than yourself. You represent the Savior, your family, your ward, your friends, and the whole Church. Make sure you fairly represent every group.

MAKING KINDERGARTEN DECISIONS

WHAT ARE KINDERGARTEN decisions? At first glance, you might think they are the decisions young children make while attending kindergarten. That is exactly correct. They are simple decisions that are vital to your success as a student or as a missionary.

There are several kindergarten decisions you need to make. I will talk about only a few and challenge you to complete the list. One decision that distinguishes "outstanding missionaries" from "ordinary missionaries" is their commitment to be obedient. This is such an elementary decision. It is easy to make and yet sometimes difficult to live. It is sort of like living the commandments Heavenly Father has given us. We should be able to live them perfectly, since no one of them is all that tough, yet we sometimes fall short. It is easy to say you will commit to being totally obedient to the mission rules. It is another battle altogether to live all the rules when you arrive in the mission. However, if you have made up your mind to be obedient, you are well on your way.

You will note I said it is easy to *make* kindergarten decisions. I never implied it would be easy to *live* those decisions. One of the decisions so easy to make and so difficult to live is getting up on time. Every morning about 6:25 A.M. (if your wake-up time is 6:30 A.M.), the devil will remind you how tired you are, how much you need another few minutes of sleep, how everybody else is sleeping in, how fifteen more minutes in bed won't make any difference. If you have made the kindergarten decision to get up on time no matter what, you will never need to make that decision again. From then on, your total energy will be directed to living the decision, not constantly remaking it.

Another kindergarten decision is to stay on your mission for the full time you were called. You are probably asking yourself why I would mention that one. It is because many missionaries begin to serve and find that a mission is more difficult than they had imagined. The devil is always there to whisper that you can't be successful, that you should just go home. This happens even to the most diligent and well-prepared of missionaries. If your decision is to serve no matter what, then you can focus all your strength on getting rid of those feelings of inadequacy. Those homesick feelings won't last long unless you waffle on the decision to stay.

Another decision is to write home once a week and to keep a journal of your mission experience. When the lure of a P-day activity hits you, you may be tempted to "postpone" writing until later. Make the kindergarten decision to write as scheduled. Then, instead of wasting valuable time debating with yourself, you will be writing letters and writing in your journal. In less time than it would take you to talk yourself out of writing, you can be finished. It is so easy to put off writing in your journal until you have a little more time. If you do, you will discover that your mission is over and you haven't recorded any of the spiritual experiences you wanted to preserve for yourself and your future family. Once the freshness of the experience is gone, you can only partially recapture your feelings. It will take only one or two missed experiences to convince you that this is one kindergarten decision you won't ever want to make again.

As a pre-missionary, you will want to make the definite decision that you will serve. Too many young men make the right decisions as a deacon, teacher, and priest only to drift into a state of indecision during their eighteenth year. If the kindergarten decision to serve was made early and kept, it will be easy to start the paperwork when the appropriate time comes. If serving a mission is top priority in your life, many of the sins that could disqualify you from serving will be much easier to resist. If serving a mission is a nonnegotiable decision, plans for work, school, and marriage will be easy to keep in proper perspective. If you don't make this kindergarten decision, most of the others won't make much difference. You can't serve an honorable mission unless you accept the call!

You can probably go through your present schedule and see many areas in which kindergarten decisions could make life much easier. The Word of Wisdom, morality, scripture reading, and church attendance are just a few that, if made correctly, free a lot of energy to use in living those commitments. Don't wait until you are nineteen or twenty-one to decide the kind of person you want to be. Remember, no one said kindergarten decisions would be easy to live; they are just easy to make. Once you have made them, the war with your unruly body still goes on, but your celestial spirit will eventually win. You will feel a lot better about yourself if you learn to make correct kindergarten decisions early and then live by them.

PREPARING FINANCIALLY

MISSIONS ARE EXPENSIVE. At the current rate of $375 a month, the cost for a sister is $6,750. For an elder who serves twenty-four months, the cost is $9,000. That sounds like a lot of money—and it is! But that isn't the entire cost. The preparation costs alone run between $1,500 and $2,000. You might be saying, "Well, Mom and Dad say they will finance my mission!" Even if they are willing, you will gain more personal reward if you pay for part of your own mission. You need to escape the childish mind-set that someone else will always pick up the tab. The missionary who pays for at least part of his or her own way is a much more diligent missionary. It is easier to waste money when it is not your own.

How much do you have to save to be prepared? That depends on how much time remains before your mission and how long you will serve. If you just turned twelve and are starting your "mission account," you would have to save about $130 a month to cover all costs for a two-year mission. If you are seventeen years old and just starting, you would have to save about $460 a month to be self-sustaining! All of a sudden, missions are really expensive! No matter how old you are or how little you have saved, you will benefit from saving as much as you can before your call comes.

Too many young people have indulged in buying expensive "toys" and then painfully discover they don't have enough money to go on a mission. Over the years, I have heard many rationalizations. One young man explained that his going into debt for a sport truck was an "investment." He planned to sell it (at a profit!) when the time for his mission arrived. But how could he know that one miscalculation on his part during his senior year of high school would leave his truck a worthless piece of junk? Comprehensive insurance coverage was too costly, so he opted for just liability insurance. Because of that, he received no money for his wrecked truck. His debt was still outstanding and had to be paid. His mission went unserved.

Cars, trucks, motorcycles, boats, jet skis, stereo systems, and the like are fun and exciting but often trap prospective missionaries in a financial maze that makes serving a mission impossible or puts an extreme hardship on Mom and Dad. Many prospective missionaries set aside 50 percent of what they earn toward their mission, and tithing takes another 10 percent, leaving 40 percent of the total to live on. That may sound like enough, but there are also taxes and various living expenses. Even if it means cutting other expenditures, don't shortchange your mission fund or the Lord (tithing).

Some rather creative young people have entered into an agreement with their parents to set aside "matching funds." For every dollar you save, Mom and Dad are willing to match it by putting a dollar in a savings account. This approach gives you the added incentive of doubling your investment. It also lessens the impact on the family budget when you leave; most of your money will already have been set aside.

As you get closer to your mission date, start buying

clothing you can use on your mission. There are limited opportunities for you to wear shorts, loud shirts, or "trendy" clothing on a mission. If you try purchasing clothing and shoes too far in advance, you may outgrow them before your mission date arrives. You might suggest to your family that Christmas, birthday, and other gifts include luggage, a camera, journals, scriptures, and other things you will need but not grow out of.

Youth is a great time of life. Buying and spending is fun and exciting. Reality is sometimes difficult to accept. Learning how to distinguish between wants and needs is an important lesson.

In addition to saving money, you will need to learn to budget the money you have. Learn to buy wisely. Start going grocery shopping with your parents. When you do, ask questions: Why did you choose this product rather than another one? Why did you buy the larger size rather than the cheaper smaller size? Why do "prepared foods" cost so much more than the ingredients to make the same thing at home? You will not have an unlimited bank account on your mission. Each mission will give you a monthly living allowance based on what the average missionary spends in that mission. If you have learned how to budget and use your funds wisely, you will have plenty. If you have not, you may find yourself without money halfway into the month. Trying to live for two weeks on starvation foods is not fun! Good budgeting makes starvation unnecessary.

Plan now to live within your allotted budget on your mission. Even if Mom and Dad can afford to send you extra money, it will be grossly unfair to the other missionaries who are not as fortunate. When you have extra money and your companion does not, it puts real stress on your companionship. Be wise enough to learn these financial practices before you leave; they will eliminate the stress of being with companions who do not know how to use their money. With proper planning now, finances will not need to become a central focus of your mission.

14

DEALING WITH GIRLFRIENDS OR BOYFRIENDS

WHILE YOU ARE on your mission, should you have a girl-friend or boyfriend waiting for you at home? Obviously, there isn't a definite answer either from the scriptures or from the Brethren. Rather, the objective is to look at the pros and cons of such a situation.

If you don't already, someday you will definitely want to have a boyfriend or girlfriend. This may or may not be the right time. Be honest and open in evaluating your situation. Sometimes, missionaries will serve with more honor because they know their special friends are keeping track of their progress. Sometimes, missionaries never quite get into their missions because they are always thinking and daydreaming about their special friends. Into which category will you fit?

If your special friend is behind you 100 percent and is willing to constantly write you encouraging letters, then maintain the relationship. If the letters are full of romantic sweet stuff, you will find it increasingly difficult to stay focused on your mission. If you are counting the days until you can be back together again, you will never get off the ground spiritually. On the other hand, if your friend helps you keep your mission and life in proper perspective, he or she may be exactly what you need to motivate you to serve more honorably.

From years of experience with elders and sisters who have left girlfriends or boyfriends behind, I would say most would have been better off had they started their missions without any social ties. The truth is that only about one out of every ten friends who are waiting for missionaries actually wait.

Talk this matter over with older brothers and sisters or friends who had someone wait. Would they do it again? Some will say yes; others will say no. At least consider the impact it will have on you if your friend decides not to wait. Will you be able to handle it? I have spent many days trying to put missionaries back together who have received the infamous "Dear John" or "Dear Jane" letters. It may be difficult to imagine your special friend writing one of those letters, but remember that all the other missionaries felt the same way before they got theirs!

There is another major consideration many premissionaries fail to take into account. For the next eighteen months or two years, you will be growing intellectually and spiritually at an incredible rate. Unless your friend is on an organized program, you will outdistance them in your progression. The result will be that although they may still like you when you get home, you may not be as interested in them. If you are planning something permanent when you return, be realistic enough to suggest a learning program for your friend: taking an institute class, teaching in the Church, doing community service, or following an individual study program—anything that will parallel what you will be doing.

Many young people do end up marrying the person who waited for them. What a great thing to have shared such a spiritual experience before you are married! Knowing that you are earning blessings for your future wife or husband and children is a real incentive to serve well (see Mark 10:28–30). And your weekly report to your friend can help keep you focused on what is really important.

If you decide to try it, set some practical and realistic guidelines. Write no more than one letter a week, which complies with the *Missionary Handbook*. If you are going to build a celestial relationship, don't try to build it on disobedience. Phone calls home are not permitted. If your mission allows calls home on Mother's Day and Christmas, then you may have the opportunity to talk *briefly* with each other. If that isn't practical, don't sacrifice the blessings promised to the faithful because of your desire to talk with each other.

Agree to focus your letters on your mission, and not on mush. Being away from each other for two years will be difficult enough without adding the burden of romantic homesickness. Share your insights into the scriptures and the gospel. Share experiences you are having as a missionary with new investigators, difficult questions, lessons you are learning, and prayers that are being answered. You will have plenty of time to catch up on the romantic side of your relationship after you get home.

Keep in mind that in spite of the best intentions of both of you, things may not work out. Make sure you do not write anything either of you will be embarrassed about if you end up marrying someone else. Several years after returning from my first mission, I met one of my missionary companions. He had been head over heels in love with his girlfriend. He would let me read some of the letters he wrote to her. I blush now as I remember some of them. She did not end up waiting for him. When he returned home (as he recounted the story), he met his ex-girlfriend, her husband, and their baby while walking down the street one day. As their eyes met, his face reddened as he remembered (and she obviously remembered) the things he had written. He said he was so embarrassed that he had consciously avoided seeing her since that time. I am so glad I didn't make the same mistake. My wife and I still enjoy visiting with my five former girlfriends and their families!

If you are just "sort of" serious, keep your relationship on a friendly note. You might have an understanding before you leave that if things don't work out, he or she will send the letters to your home as another record of your mission. Knowing that your future spouse and children might read the letters will also help you keep the relationship on a friendly plane.

If you decide the "waiting game" isn't right for you, break off your relationship carefully. You still don't know what the future may hold. You may have second thoughts later on. If so, you'll be glad you didn't burn your bridges behind you. It is such a relief to begin serving your mission without regrets about the relationships you had before you left home.

If things don't work out, agree to be friends. Those same qualities that attracted you to each other before your mission may well be the qualities your future "friends" will have. Don't act like a child if waiting doesn't work out. Since I have had to counsel many missionaries on the matter, I will also counsel you: Don't continue to correspond after your special friend is someone else's wife or husband! Those first months of marriage are a big enough adjustment without the added irritation from continued correspondence. It's funny how something that obvious escapes so many!

One more consoling thought: Although your boyfriend

or girlfriend might end up marrying someone else while you are serving your mission, your husband or wife will not! Trust the Lord. You are on his errand, and he will watch out for you.

Waiting itself is neither positive nor negative. How you deal with it makes all the difference in the world.

LEAVING THE PAST BEHIND

ONLY ONE PERSON HAS LED A perfect life. As good as your mother thinks you are, that One isn't you! Since all have made mistakes, it almost becomes a game with some missionaries to talk, sometimes in a boasting way, about things they have done wrong. When you go to talk with the bishop and clear up the past, that should bury it once and for all. Don't keep bringing it up over and over.

There are good reasons to let the past stay buried. You are going to be held up as an example of what every mother and father wants their son or daughter to be. Bringing up the past gives the people who are listening to you a license to do the same thing. They will be saying in their minds, "Wow, Elder or Sister Jones sure is a neat person. If they could sin before their mission and still turn out good, maybe I can do the same thing!" Since people see you only the way you are now, they will not be aware of how much you suffered and learned as you repented. If you have really repented of your sins, you will wish you had never done them. You will look back with regret and pray mightily that the Lord will never bring them back. And you certainly won't boast about them.

If you become aware now that others look to you as an example, it will be easier when your conservative clothes and name tag label you as a Mormon missionary. Do you know that some of the kids in your neighborhood look at you and want to grow up to be like you? From the day you come out of the waters of baptism until the day you die, you can never escape being a living testimony. Either your good example will bear testimony of the Lord and his church, or your bad example will bear testimony of Satan and his counterfeit gospel. You are the only one who can choose for which side you will bear your testimony. You cannot choose whether or not to be a living testimony. You can only choose between being a good or bad example.

Use this simple key to help you know whether you are dressing, acting, and talking appropriately: *If attention is drawn to you and away from your message, you are doing or wearing something inappropriate.* For example, if a priest were to bless the sacrament while wearing an earring, people in the congregation might focus more on the earring than on the Savior. You might think the problem lies with everyone else, but it doesn't. You are commissioned by priesthood ordinance to stand in the place of the Savior to the people. You are not authorized to do anything that would distract them from following the Savior.

Mistakes you have made in the past are not anything of which you should be proud. When you truly repent, you crucify the "old man of sin" (see Romans 6:6) and put on the new man in Christ. Someday, unless you continue to remind the Lord about those mistakes, he will "remember them no more" (D&C 58:42). Why chance having them continually remembered by constantly talking about them? The Lord remembers them no more unless you choose to bring them up.

16

GIVING IT YOUR ALL

THE PREPARATION PERIOD, the Missionary Training Center, and the farewell scene at the airport will have you so pumped you will hardly be able to contain yourself. Those things have announced that you are now actually starting the service everyone has talked so much about and for which you have waited so long. This enthusiasm will carry you for the first month of your mission. However, you must realize that difficult times await you, so don't be surprised when they hit.

Unfortunately, too many missionaries become overwhelmed with the amount of work there is to do and get discouraged. Some resign themselves to just enduring to the end, while others realize the responsibility they took on when they accepted the call and roll up their sleeves to do as much as they can. There are definite rewards for working hard in spite of what others may do. There is also a sobering caution given to us by President Joseph Fielding Smith:

> [Missionaries] were to remember . . . one important duty which they were to fulfill and that was to be sure and bear testimony in every instance. If they performed their labors sincerely, humbly and diligently bearing witness of the restoration then it would be more tolerable for the heathen in the day of judgment, than for

that house which rejected the message. If no warning had been left, however, then the judgment would be pronounced against the servant who was expected to deliver it. . . . The elders who delivered the message were also to be judges in the day of judgment against those who rejected their testimony. Missionaries of the Church should realize this fact. They are sent to warn the world and when they faithfully do their duty they will stand as witnesses against those who reject them, but if they fail to perform their duty, then those unto whom the message should have been given, will stand up as accusers in their turn, and the unfaithful servants will be condemned. (*Church History and Modern Revelation* [Salt Lake City: The Church of Jesus Christ of Latter-day Saints, 1946], p. 47)

Think of it: a price must be paid for the testimony you will bear. If you faithfully do your duty, it won't make any difference (to you) whether the people accept or reject your testimony. You will be blessed as though everyone you teach joined the Church. However, if you fail to bear your testimony every opportunity you have, then the people you should have warned will stand to condemn you in the day of judgment. Knowing this, can you see how essential it is to be faithful and diligent in doing what you have been called to do?

On June 7, 1962, President Henry D. Moyle addressed missionaries in California about being diligent during their missions:

I shall go to my grave saying that missionaries . . . never rise in their entire life above the stature they carve out for themselves in the mission field. I ask the missionaries all over the world to write that in their book, and then read the book ten years from now. If perchance, they have not risen in that first ten years after they come home from the mission field, above that status of mediocrity that they (may have) maintained in the mission field, (they should) get down on their knees, pray, and work a little harder and seek to overcome that tremendous handicap they placed upon themselves by their lack of application, lack of appreciation, and lack of dedication in the mission field.

This is your opportunity for greatness. The rewards for faithful service will set the course for the rest of your life. If you really want to excel and become great, don't cheat yourself and the Lord by serving a casual mission. You have heard many times the saying that has been printed on posters, cross-stitched on wall hangings, and imprinted on pocket-sized reminder cards: "I never said it would be easy. I just said it would be worth it!" For missionaries, that is a true statement indeed!

It is not *what* but *who* that determines the success of your mission. The obvious answer is *you*. If you will decide now to take advantage of every opportunity to share the gospel and bear your testimony, you will be laying the foundation of greatness in your life. Since not all your companions and other missionaries may share your attitude, you have the opportunity to help them catch the same vision. President Smith's and President Moyle's statements are intended for the entire missionary force. What a blessing you will be to your mission and the Lord when you faithfully share the gospel with everyone you meet!

As a preparing missionary, you can learn to be diligent and faithful. Start now by concentrating on the present. Too many missionaries (and others) constantly look to the future as a time when they will finally be "happy." Others insist on talking endlessly about experiences they have enjoyed or endured in the past. What a terrible waste to be constantly "wishing away" your mission! Waiting until you are a senior companion or a leader or until your mission will be over is fruitless and even counterproductive. I have comforted many missionaries who thought happiness would come the last day of their mission. But only then did they discover they had fallen in love with the work, the gospel, the people, and the area. They realized too late that they did not want to leave.

You can't do much about the past. It is gone and can't be recalled. The future will arrive one moment at a time, but when it does, it is called "the present." If you are still in school, concentrate on enjoying each class period. It may be difficult in some instances. But if you can learn now to look for the good, the pleasurable, or the principle you are to learn, then the time will pass more quickly, and you will not look back with regret at having wasted part of your life. You may have a job before your mission. Practice being the best employee you can be. Don't worry too much about whether you are being paid what you think you are worth or whether the job is boring or difficult or unrewarding. Learning how to give an honest day's work for a day's pay will get you into the habit of serving with total honor. Don't make excuses for skipping work. If you are genuinely sick, call and let your employer know you won't be in. If you are just not motivated to go to work—go anyway. Happiness does not depend on a certain environment or activity. Happiness is a state of mind over which you have complete control. If you are not happy, don't fall into the satanic trap of blaming someone else. Take stock of where you are and the direction you are going; make a change if necessary. Life can be thrilling and rewarding, unless we wait around for someone else to tailor-make the environment to our liking.

You will hear it over and over again: "A mission is either the best or the worst time of your life. It all depends on you." How true that is! Being in the habit of taking full advantage of every moment, working as hard and as efficiently as you know how, and consciously enjoying each moment—these will create a memory of your mission you will relish forever. Live each moment now.

17

LEARNING TO TALK TO ADULTS

OVER THE YEARS, I HAVE NOTICED how children seem to go
through stages. When we were little, we were afraid of "big
people" and shyly said nothing. As we grew older, we became
more aware of those around us. Adults may have viewed us
as obnoxious or a pain. As we matured toward adulthood, we
may have gone through a second "shy" stage and again chose
to be silent. Why do we clam up when adults are around? Are
we afraid our ideas may sound silly or childish? Whatever the
reason may be, you need to overcome shyness before going
on your mission.

In doing a self-inventory, see if you are comfortable in
discussing a variety of issues with adults. Do you wait for
them to start the conversation? Do you answer in monosyl-
lables? Do you look down or away when someone is talking
to you directly? Do you stutter or stumble when trying to
answer a question? If you do any of these, you can overcome
them with a little practice.

Choose someone you respect and trust. Ask him or her
to help you learn to express yourself. Choose a topic in which
you may differ in your beliefs. Practice expressing yourself
clearly and forcefully on this topic without being overbearing. Have the person critique your abilities. Learn to accept

the person's criticism. Watch people who successfully do the things you are trying to learn.

If you are still going to school, think about taking a class in speech or debate. But be cautious on your mission about trying to use *all* you learn in debate. "Bashing" or arguing will not bring the Spirit but will result in far fewer converts than you might otherwise get. Learn to ask and answer questions in class. You will find classes in school much more interesting if you are involved than if you wait around for the teacher to "entertain" you. Hearing yourself ask intelligent questions will give you confidence in your intellectual abilities. Asking questions also gives you a nonthreatening opportunity to see how people react to you. If the class gets upset because of your questions, you may be using the wrong tone of voice. Ask, don't challenge! If the teacher asks you repeatedly to "rephrase the question," you can bet you are not making yourself clearly understood. Learn to speak loudly enough so the person you are addressing can easily hear you and not have to guess at what you are saying. In other words, "Don't mumble!"

Listen to the news often enough to be able to discuss intelligently what is happening in the world. Don't be so quick to label as "worthless" the classes you are taking in school. The Lord gave us a rather lengthy list of subjects with which we ought to be familiar when we go on our missions:

Teach ye diligently [we could also say "discuss"] and my grace shall attend you, that you may be instructed more perfectly in theory [an educated guess on how things might work], in principle [a fundamental truth on which other laws are based], in doctrine [something taught, especially as the principles or beliefs of a religion], in the law of the gospel, in all things that pertain unto the kingdom of God, that are expedient for you to understand; of things both in heaven [astronomy] and in the earth [agriculture, forestry, ecology], and under the earth [mineralogy, geology]; things which have been [history], things which are [current events], things which must shortly come to pass [prophecies]; things which are at home [domestic affairs], things which are abroad [foreign affairs]; the wars and the perplexities of the nations [politics], and the judgments which are on the land [floods, droughts, famines, plagues, diseases, crime waves]; and a knowledge also of countries and of kingdoms [geography, political science, sociology, economics]—[For what purpose?] That ye may be prepared in all things when I shall send you again to magnify the calling whereunto I have called you, and the mission with which I have commissioned you. (D&C 88:78–80)

You will not master these topics by watching television comedy! Still, many wonderful television documentaries and science shows may add to your understanding. It is much easier to talk to people you will meet on your mission if you know at least a little about a great many topics. If you are totally unprepared in the areas the Lord has outlined, you will be more afraid to talk to "educated" adults.

Learn before your mission to graciously remain silent when someone strongly disagrees with your point of view. During your mission, you may encounter people who would love to draw you into a verbal (sometimes physical) fight over your beliefs. If you have learned self-control, you will not be so foolish as to engage in bashing with them.

Don't be afraid someone will disprove the Church; the Church is true. You may not know the immediate answer to every question thrown your way, but you can rest assured Heavenly Father knows the answer and has promised to tell you what *he* wants people to know in the very moment you need the answer. He said, "Neither take ye thought beforehand what ye shall say; but *treasure up in your minds continually* the words of life, and it shall be given you in the very hour that portion that shall be meted unto every man" (D&C 84:85; emphasis added). Another declaration by the Lord confirms this promise: "Lift up your voices unto this people; speak the thoughts that I shall put into your hearts, and you shall not be confounded before men; for it shall be given you in the very hour, yea, in the *very moment,* what ye shall say" (D&C 100:5–6; emphasis added). From thousands of experiences, both my own and those reported to me by missionaries, I know these promises are true. Do yourself a favor and "treasure up continually the words of life" and see if the Lord doesn't do the same for you.

You will understand more about the gospel after you have gained some teaching experience. But in spite of the little you know, it is many times more than your investigators know. Your understanding of what certain passages mean may silence even learned ministers. Read carefully what the Lord said about you as a missionary: "I, the Lord, am merciful and gracious unto those who fear me, and delight to honor those who serve me in righteousness and in truth unto the end. And their wisdom shall be great, and their understanding reach to heaven; and before them the wisdom of the wise shall perish, and the understanding of the prudent shall come to naught. For by my Spirit will I enlighten them" (D&C 76:5, 9, 10).

You may naturally feel timid or shy around those of greater age and education than yourself. Nevertheless, the

Lord expects you to be tactfully bold in your teaching. In fact, he chastised elders in the early days of the Church for being afraid to talk: "With some I am not well pleased, for they will not open their mouths, but they hide the talent which I have given unto them, because of the fear of man. Wo unto such, for mine anger is kindled against them" (D&C 60:2).

Practice discussing eternal truths before you go on your mission; it will save you a lot of grief and anxiety when you arrive. Start today talking, discussing, presenting, listening, studying, asking, and answering topics that require spiritual understanding.

18

LEARNING SELF-CONTROL

Our MODERN SOCIETY TEACHES that a real man never walks away from a fight. But the Lord has asked us to turn the other cheek and control our actions. At times during your mission, people may push you to the limit. How you react can make the difference in whether a person does or doesn't join the Church.

One muscular Tongan elder shared an experience of self-control during a zone conference. This 230-pound elder and his equally muscular companion were being physically threatened and verbally abused by a 120-pound man. The abuser grabbed the Tongan by the tie and put his face right in the elder's face. The man swore and yelled, letting the elders know what sissies he thought they were and how much he hated Mormons. He threatened them and commanded them to leave immediately or he would "chew them up and spit them out." When the Tongan elder asked how he thought he would do that, the man demonstrated his defiance by biting the missionary's bicycle tire. How easy it would have been for the elder to "dispose" of this man. How grateful he was that he didn't. After the harassment, which lasted for about ten minutes, the detractor left, muttering oaths and curses to himself. As the missionaries turned to continue on their way, they saw a group of fifty people who had gathered to watch their reaction to the situation. They later taught many discussions to people from that group, and several of the people were eventually baptized. If these elders had not learned to control themselves before their missions, they might have damaged the good reputation of the Church and the missionary program. But they had previously learned to take charge of a situation and not to respond to every little irritation by fighting or yelling.

Some elders have not learned the valuable lessons of self-control and calmly walking away from confrontations. Such missionaries should take a crash course in self-control so they don't embarrass themselves, the mission, and the Church.

Controlling your temper is only one of many important areas of self-control. Controlling your appetite is also a must. Many places in the world teeter on the brink of famine. So if you eat without considering who else needs to eat, others may be forced to go without food. I learned this lesson the hard way. As young missionaries in Samoa, we had just experienced the first of three major hurricanes that destroyed our food supply. We had been invited to a meal with a member some distance from our home. By the time we arrived, I was famished. It seemed like forever since I had enjoyed a good meal. The food was brought and laid before us. After the blessing, I dived in, trying to satisfy my gnawing hunger. I devoured every scrap of food on the plate. Then I noticed my companion had only nibbled at his food. I thought he was crazy. I even thought of offering to finish his food if he didn't want it. Then I saw the look of disgust on his face. Without a word, he motioned toward a group of children watching us from the far side of the room. It took a few seconds for the reality of the situation to dawn on me: the only food they would be eating is what we didn't eat! I felt sick. Many times during the rest of my mission, I learned to suppress my hunger because many little mouths would appreciate my control.

Controlling your mind is another essential trait to learn. Many places in the world have a different standard of modesty than we do in the United States. That doesn't make them either good or bad—just different. If you have not learned to control your eyes and your thoughts, you could be in real trouble. Develop a system for keeping your mind clean. Learn to use Satan against Satan. Whenever you are tempted to entertain bad thoughts, use the temptation as a catalyst to remind you to think and do something righteous: memorize a scripture, read a chapter from the Book of Mormon, say a prayer, sing a favorite hymn, recite an uplifting poem, or do a service project. Any of these things will quickly put you in control of your mind and rescue you from the tempter. You will soon discover that Satan is not stupid; he just isn't intelligent! He will say, "Wait a minute. When I tempt Elder Jones, he is not tempted and actually does something that takes him further away from my kingdom." Satan will then withdraw the temptations in those areas (and hit you from a different direction). You can control your mind if you really try.

As teenagers, we are sometimes foolish enough to take a dare and do something we would normally never consider. We might even be called "chicken," "wimp," or "mama's boy" if we refuse. Learn to ignore the taunting. Satan has his mortal imps who will try to lure you into verbal or physical combat by using vulgarity or calling you names. If you have mastered the talent of walking away, it will be easy to continue. If you have the reputation of never walking away from a good fight, you will be in trouble. After a couple of incidents of fighting, your right to continue serving as a missionary will be brought into question. Don't allow Satan to destroy your mission because of your failure to control yourself.

19

SERVING FOR THE RIGHT REASONS

DOESN'T EVERYONE go on a mission to serve the Lord? It would be wonderful if everyone did. Probably any reason for going on a mission is a good reason *if* you end up getting converted after you get there. But you and the mission will benefit more if you determine to go to serve others and not just to serve yourself. If you happen to learn and grow (which you undoubtedly will) as a result of your service, that is fine. But when you go to serve, be willing to do whatever the mission president and the Lord ask. A self-serving attitude will make you angry and discouraged when you don't get the position you want or don't get to serve where you want.

Attitudes can be altered. You may have developed an "attitude" over your lifetime. But since a mission is such a great time of change anyway, you might consider an attitude adjustment before you go. To determine if you may have the wrong attitude for a mission, ask yourself, "If I am never called to a position of leadership in my mission, will I consider myself a failure?" If the answer is yes, you need to ask, "Who am I going to serve, myself or the Lord?" Remember, during his mortal ministry the Savior was never a district leader, a zone leader, or an assistant. He was a servant to all!

Some young men go on missions because their girlfriends won't marry anyone but a returned missionary. That's a good choice for the girls but a terrible misunderstanding to believe that simply being away from home for two years constitutes serving a mission. Again, you might ask yourself, "If my friend ends up not waiting for me, will I still be willing to serve a mission?" If the answer is no, you ought to adjust your point of view. There is about a 90 percent chance your special someone will not wait for you.

A few young men serve because a relative has promised them the car or truck of their choice when they return from their mission. My experience with such missionaries has been one of frustration and disappointment—unless they adjust their attitude. Missionary work is too difficult and too sacred to do just to earn a car. Although you might receive various gifts when you return, the most valuable gifts will be your spiritual growth, the eternal lessons you've learned, and the principles of successful living you have mastered as a result of your Christlike service. Ask yourself, "If no one gives me anything or even says thanks for my service, would I still be enthusiastic about serving?" If not, change your attitude.

Some young people decide to serve because their family expects it of them. Grandfather served, father served, older brothers and sisters have served, and now it's their turn. That is a good tradition, but it certainly is not the correct reason to serve. Serving a mission puts you in a select group of faithful Latter-day Saints. Some people may mock you for going, but those who ridicule have never served missions themselves. There are many reasons for serving a mission. For example, unexpected blessings will come to your family because of your service, but that should not be the determining factor. You may also be the first to serve from your family, or the hundredth. Ask yourself, "If no one in my family cares either way, would I still go?" If the answer is no, you need an attitude adjustment.

Some young people go because their friends may be going, so they had better go too. That is a powerful but temporary reason to go, because missionaries soon realize that the rigors of missionary life rapidly overcome the social push to serve. Certainly having friends serve throughout the world is a wonderful thing. Letters comparing and contrasting missions are motivating and exciting. I remember living on coconut and raw fish (because our food supply had been wiped out by a hurricane), and my friend in Chile wrote me about eating steak and strawberry pie. The exchange of letters helped us both through some difficult times, and we have laughed about and enjoyed sharing stories ever since we returned twenty-five years ago. So ask yourself, "If none of my friends go on missions, would I still go?" If the answer is no—you guessed it—you need an attitude change.

A few young people go on a mission because they didn't get accepted into school, their girlfriend or boyfriend just dumped them, or they can't think of anything else to do. Serving a full-time mission is one of the most honorable and valuable experiences God has provided for his children. So a mission should not be used as a second-option plan. Nevertheless, many of these young people eventually catch the vision of a mission and serve with honor and diligence. Unfortunately, some never catch on and become a dead weight to companions and the mission leadership.

Many young men serve because "the prophet has asked every worthy young man to serve." This noble reason is one of the better ones, because that kind of dedication will carry them a long way in life. It is difficult to fault a young man or young woman for responding to such a noble call. But this response is a distant second to the best reason: you should go because you love God and his Son and want to share their wonderful gospel with your spiritual brothers and sisters. When someone rejects your divine message, if you are there for any reason other than selfless service for the Savior, it will likely result in discouragement and depression. But when people reject your message and your mission centered on Christ, they are only rejecting him. You feel sorry that they are not willing to follow him and gain eternal life, but the presence of his Spirit replaces any feelings of personal rejection you may have. A powerful commentary is given in 3 Nephi 28:34–35: "Wo be unto him that will not hearken unto the words of Jesus, and also to them whom he hath chosen and sent among them; for whoso receiveth not the words of Jesus and the words of those whom he hath sent receiveth not him; and therefore he will not receive them at the last day; and it would be better for them if they had not been born."

Even in the powerful oath and covenant of the priesthood, the Lord reveals, "He that receiveth my servants receiveth me" (D&C 84:36).

Going on a mission for the right reason is like shooting at the bull's-eye of a target. It is much more likely you will hit the mark if you aim right than to assume that just by firing your rifle you might hit the bull's-eye. Before you ever get to your mission area, do whatever attitude adjustment is necessary to make sure you are serving for the right reason.

20

DECIDING TO BE OBEDIENT

YOU LIVE IN AN INTERESTING world. Your parents shake their heads in disbelief at your generation. But most likely, their parents (your grandparents) were equally shocked at how permissive the world was when your parents were growing up. However, some disturbing trends have surfaced in your day that should cause everyone a great deal of concern: the suffering and total disregard of human life caused by lawless gangs, the wholesale destruction of an entire generation of young people by the use of illegal drugs, and the general disregard of law and order.

Being born and raised in this kind of environment makes it difficult not to be affected. During your high school days, cheating may have been a way of passing classes. For many, lying has become just another form of speech, and selective obedience is often considered a component of being "smart." As you prepare to serve a mission, you need to consider carefully your attitude toward obeying the commandments. If you feel you have the right to select which mission rules you keep and which ones you don't, you are setting yourself up for a mediocre mission at best. The Lord never did say: "I, the Lord, am bound if ye do 80 percent of what I say." He has promised, "I, the Lord, am bound when ye do [100 percent of] what I say; but when ye do not what I say, ye have no promise" (D&C 82:10). Obedience is a decision. Make it only once. Never entertain Satan's temptations to revise a previously made decision every time a new situation arises. If the Lord commands, do it. You will do yourself a huge favor by starting to strengthen your obedient attitude *before* your mission. When the Lord asks you to home teach, go every month. Right now you may have two or three families to visit. In many areas of the world where home teaching is just getting started or where the priesthood leaders use missionaries to find the lost or less-active, you may have twenty or thirty families to visit! These months or years before your mission should be used to learn, on a small scale, what habits and traits missionaries need on a large scale.

Since the Lord has asked you to attend your meetings, go every week without fail. It was always a shock and disappointment to hear the elder or sister who had only recently become active in the Church complain about all the meetings missionaries have to attend. Right now you attend the block meetings, maybe a Bishop's Youth Council, and perhaps a fireside on Sunday. As a missionary you will be required to attend, participate in, and conduct various meetings. For example, you may attend a correlation meeting with the ward mission leaders from wards where you serve, participate in two three-hour block meetings, and conduct two or three firesides all in one week. It is not at all unusual for missionaries to be in different meetings from 6:30 A.M. to 8:30 P.M. on Sundays, without a break! What a shock to your system if you think a seventy-minute sacrament meeting is long.

A mission requires you to be in control of yourself. If you have developed the habit of doing whatever you please until somebody puts the stops on you, you may find it difficult to control yourself during your mission. Start now to do what you know you should, whether somebody is watching you or not. A friend of mine, who was recently released as a mission president, shared the following story. He once overheard a conversation between two high school seniors who did not know he was listening. They were boasting about how they had really pulled the wool over their English teacher's eyes by faking it through her class without learning how to read. One said he had never learned to read during the full twelve years of school. To my friend's surprise, the "nonreader" was eventually assigned to the mission over which he presided. To the missionary's eternal credit, he did eventually learn to read. But he experienced many uncomfortable and embarrassing situations as he crammed years of study into a few months. Many times, my friend thought to himself, "Yes, you really did pull the wool over your teacher's eyes. But you are the one who now must pay the terrible price."

If we could just learn now that we never "get away with" anything! Every choice has a consequence we cannot escape. Every time we willingly disobey, the consequence will eventually catch up with us. It is childish to think we can pick up one end of a stick and get the other end of a different stick. If you pick up good study habits, you will eventually gain knowledge and understanding. If you pick up cheating, short-cutting, and responsibility dodging, you will eventually get disappointment, and the loss of the Spirit.

You may find yourself, as I did, hundreds of miles from the mission headquarters on an island with only you and your companion. Nobody will check up on you; no one will see if you get up on time, go to bed on time, or do any work—no one, that is, but your Heavenly Father. By the presence or absence of his Spirit, I learned to recognize that unseen eyes are always on us and are taking careful notes that will be used to our honor or our discredit at the day of judgment. Both as a young missionary and as a mission president, I am glad I made the decision to be obedient, even when nobody was there to check on me. Although I made many mistakes, I was diligent enough to enjoy the companionship of the Holy Ghost. This gift is denied to those who decide to revise the decision of obedience with every changing situation.

21

DEVELOPING EMOTIONAL STABILITY

HIGH SCHOOL IS PROBABLY THE best training ground for the emotional roller coaster called a mission. In high school, one day can be wonderful because you won a football game, and the next day can be depressing because you didn't get a date to a dance. Mission life also has its ups and downs. Unfortunately during high school, we may not have reacted in an adult manner to these fluctuations. If you are accustomed to falling to pieces over mounting frustrations, you need to change your reaction.

Only you can determine your emotional stability. The world suggests that your environment makes all the difference. Although environment can contribute to your happiness or sadness, it does not have the power to control you. On your mission, you may find yourself in some deplorable situations and end up enjoying them. If you determine you are going to eliminate the extreme highs and the depressing lows from your mood swings, you will be a stable missionary. Just refuse to let yourself be easily swayed by what is going on around you.

You probably know people who always seem happy. Why don't you ask them how they do it? No matter what happens, they always look for the good, and everything eventually seems to turn out well for them. Others are just the opposite. No matter how much they have or how well things are going for them, they always look for, and usually find, the negative. When success comes during a test or on the athletic field, they always warn about the impending failure the next time. It is difficult to be around people who concentrate on the negative.

If you are one of those people, how do you go about changing? Recognizing you have a problem is a step in the right direction. Decide to eliminate the negative words from your vocabulary: *can't, don't, fail, quit,* and *lose.* Start looking for the good in everything. If you lose a ball game, you will know what you need to improve before the next game. If you get turned down for a date, determine what characteristics make you less than desirable and begin to change them.

Start listening to others. You will be surprised how negative people are. Negative attitudes are depressing. You don't want to go around depressed all the time, so avoid the "negative trap." Try to interject something positive into every conversation. If your entire group is negative, they will look at you as if something is wrong. Being around such people is like being in a room that is totally dark. Everyone is comfortable in the dark (because they don't know any better) until someone brings a light into the room. After that, they are not content to be in the dark. You will be surprised how quickly you can get others to join you in being more positive. You are to be a light to the world (see 3 Nephi 12:14).

You will need all the practice you can get. During your mission, many factors could contribute to your having a negative attitude. If you have learned to share your positive light with others before your mission, you will find it easier to do so during your mission. The simple but accurate adage applies: "Whether you think you can or you can't, you are correct!"

Determine the kinds of things that cause you to have a negative attitude. Is it when you are rejected when asking for a date? When you don't make the team? When you fail a test? Rejection can be almost hour by hour in missionary service. People do not often reject you as a person, but they may reject what you stand for and whom you represent. If you haven't learned to deal with rejection before you go, you could easily get depressed on your mission. Practice controlling how you react to rejection. Life still goes on, even if your invitation to go on a date is refused. The world won't end if you don't make the team or if you fail a test. Fifty years from now, you won't even remember the teacher's name, let alone the questions you missed on the test.

Next, look at your reaction to rejection. If you pout, throw a temper tantrum, storm off, lash out, or emotionally break down, then you need to take control of yourself. None of those responses are acceptable for missionaries. You won't need to seek out emotional stress to practice your controlling techniques—stress will find you! Trials are just a part of life; we will never escape them completely. Each time you face a situation that has caused you problems, take positive action to stay happy and even tempered. Also, don't lose your self-control when things are going well. Obnoxious and over-animated responses often upset people, so control your extreme reactions. When you get into situations in which you normally run away, try staying and rationally talking through the problem. It will surprise and please those who differ with you. Learn to know your limits. If you really are losing control and you can't help it, find an acceptable way to release some pressure. Knocking a hole in the wall with your fist is not acceptable at home or on a mission. Maybe lifting weights or running or talking through the problem with a friend will have the same pressure-reducing results.

If you feel like crying all the time, you may need some additional help. Unfortunately, the world does not slow down to give you a rest, and the pace of a mission is demanding. There just isn't much time to stand back and regroup. However, prayer will greatly help you to put your problems into proper perspective. Give the Lord a chance to help you learn more about yourself. You need to learn some strategies to help you cope with the stress. If necessary, seek the advice of a professional with your parents or priesthood leader. Since the Lord knows how difficult it is to live in these latter days, he has provided a good support system to help us emotionally cope with our ever-changing situations.

Childish behavior is hard to deal with both at home and on a mission. Learning to recognize these childish traits and overcoming them will help you be a more effective mission- ary and leader. The fact that life is full of struggles doesn't mean you can't overcome them. Don't assume that your problems will just disappear on your mission; every emotion is greatly intensified in missionary service. Get control of yourself now.

Identifying and Overcoming Goliaths

Everyone has character weaknesses that need to be overcome. If you are totally honest in evaluating your present condition, you will recognize the need to change before you enter the celestial kingdom. Just like David the shepherd boy, who had to overcome the giant Goliath, so too will you have giants to conquer. What kinds of things are considered "Goliaths?" You could make a long list, but let me share how I identified my first major challenge.

I was sitting on a beach in Samoa just watching the waves pound across the reef. My companion was resting against a palm tree not too far away. I started thinking about the celestial kingdom: "What things are you doing that you know you will have to change before you will be welcome in the presence of God?" I suddenly realized one of my main weaknesses: I was notorious for sulking. Whenever something didn't go just right, I would go silent. Maybe you do the same thing. But I had perfected the fault. So I made a conscious decision to overcome that un-Christlike habit. It didn't happen all at once. But over several months, I started to control my silence. Before the end of my mission, I felt I had pretty well overcome the problem. Although challenged frequently when I returned home, I remembered how good it felt to be in control of my attitude. I would just say to myself, "No, you are not going to wimp out and sulk. That is selfish and un-Christlike, and you can control it." Then I would force myself to smile, talk, engage in conversation, or do something physically active. Miraculously, the inclination to sulk eventually disappeared. Each time I mastered the inclination to sulk, the urge got weaker and weaker. Every time I suppressed the desire to be silent, the urge became less frequent. Even today, I have to watch myself, but I know it isn't impossible to control my attitude.

Some psychologists and others say we are a product of our environment, and they put tags and labels on our unacceptable behavior, giving it a technical name and thereby making it "okay" to engage in it. You will find yourself soaring spiritually if you refuse to accept your undesirable traits and try diligently to overcome them. Some traits may require professional help or medication to control. But I am convinced that these are few and far between when we finally decide to improve.

Don't be discouraged if your lifelong habit is difficult to break. You may have a short fuse on your temper. Learning to control yourself and control the elements that have traditionally set you off is a rewarding experience. As you gain mastery over your temper, the Spirit will let you know that God is pleased with your efforts and will help you.

The Lord has put our weaknesses and problems in a whole new perspective: "If men come unto me I will show unto them their weakness. *I give unto men weakness* that they may be humble; and my grace is sufficient for all men that humble themselves before me; for if they humble themselves before me, and have faith in me, then will I make weak things become strong unto them" (Ether 12:27; emphasis added). Since the Lord gives us weaknesses, he has promised to help us overcome them—we don't have to do it on our own. He will make our weaknesses become strengths if we will follow some simple steps:

1. Identify the characteristic or personality flaw you want to overcome.

2. Go to the Lord in prayer and explain what you want to overcome. Ask for his help. According to his promise, he will show you how to overcome the problem.

3. Think about the problem.

4. List any positive steps you might take to help overcome the problem.

5. Take action. Consciously get involved with improving yourself and reach your expectations. Also, don't be afraid to ask your parents, friends, and leaders for help or advice.

The more you practice, the easier it will be to overcome the problem. Do not focus on the problem all the time, however. The Savior has taught us an interesting concept: "Whosoever will save his life shall lose it: and whosoever will lose his life for my sake shall find it" (Matthew 16:25). If we focus on ourselves, we lose our spiritual substance, which is the real definition of a person. When you forget about yourself (lose yourself), your spiritual self begins to grow. It becomes easier to find yourself because there is more of you to find. Try it, and you will find that the Savior speaks the truth.

Many young people need to overcome the "Goliath" of being obnoxious. Whether they do it to get attention or because they don't know how to act appropriately, it needs to be overcome. Watch people's reactions to your behavior. If they look shocked or annoyed, *you need to change.* You are wrong if you think it is their problem if they don't like the way you act. You are sent to serve and bring people to the Savior. You can't do that if your behavior or attitude drives them away.

Another "Goliath" may be personal hygiene. Showering, using deodorant, brushing your teeth, changing your socks, grooming neatly, and clearing up your complexion—all will help you present a more acceptable image. Identifying and eliminating nervous tics or unconscious habits will also help. In a class I took on student teaching, we were required to teach a lesson before a group of our classmates. The presentation was to be videotaped so we could review it. We had been cautioned beforehand to make sure we were properly dressed, zipped up, well groomed, and relaxed. One young man was so worried his pants were unzipped that he raised and lowered his zipper a dozen times during a presentation. He was totally unaware of his actions. When he saw the replay, he dropped the class and changed his major. One young missionary had to be corrected many times before he broke the nervous habit of picking his nose.

If you have a habit of interrupting people as they speak, work on not doing it. If you refuse to make eye contact during a conversation, practice until you have mastered doing so.

As you overcome your weaknesses, you will begin to anticipate the challenge of tackling another one. It becomes like a game. Instead of worrying about not being perfect, you will begin looking forward to the challenge. "Give me another mountain!" is the attitude. Happy is the missionary who is in the habit of identifying and overcoming his giants. If you can overcome the most noticeable and annoying habits before you start your mission, the others will be readily overcome. You will not become perfect before you get your call or after your call. Don't worry—you will always have something to work on during your mission. If you postpone correcting your "Goliaths" until you start your mission, you may be embarrassed because of your weaknesses and waste the Lord's time correcting them.

GOING FORTH WITH HONOR

WHERE WILL YOU BE CALLED to serve? It will be no surprise to the Lord, although it may be a surprise to you. You were called before the foundations of this earth to serve a mission. The place doesn't make a difference, but how you serve makes all the difference in the world. The Prophet Joseph Smith taught, "Every man who has a calling to minister to the inhabitants of the world was ordained to that very purpose in the Grand Council of heaven before this world was" (*Teachings of the Prophet Joseph Smith*, comp. Joseph Fielding Smith [Salt Lake City: Deseret Book Co., 1938], p. 365). So your decision to serve is just the final preparatory step to something you have been waiting to do for thousands of years. No wonder you are excited!

Some missionaries make the mistake of wanting to tell the Lord where they should serve. Resist the temptation. He knows you better than you know yourself. He has prepared people for you to touch whom no one else can touch. He knows everything about your mission. Let him be the Lord and you be content to be his servant. If you are assigned to a mission and circumstances require a change, don't feel as if you are letting the Lord down. I learned a valuable lesson when President Gordon B. Hinckley called Sister Bott and me to our mission. After President Hinckley issued the call, I asked where we would be serving. He replied, "President Bott, the world is a big place. Where you are assigned to serve doesn't make a difference. That may change half a dozen times before you end up where you are going to serve. The important thing is that you have been called."

Young missionaries receive a letter that calls them to serve and assigns them to a certain mission area, so it is easy to make the mistake of saying, "I was called to the Samoan Mission." More correctly they should say, "I was called as a missionary and assigned to work in Samoa." Throughout your mission, your specific assignments may change. Usually it is within the mission boundaries. Occasionally, demands and circumstances will dictate that you receive a "special transfer" to a different mission or a different language. But your call as a missionary never changes.

What a thrill to be invited to serve on the Lord's first team during the last minutes of the fourth quarter of the greatest game ever played! President Ezra Taft Benson gave a stirring address on realizing who you are and what an honor it is to serve now:

> For nearly six thousand years, God has held you in reserve to make your appearance in the final days before the Second Coming of the Lord. . . . While our generation will be comparable in wickedness to the days of Noah, when the Lord cleansed the earth by flood, there is a major difference this time. It is that God has saved for the final inning some of his strongest children, who will help bear off the Kingdom triumphantly. And that is where you come in, for you are the generation that must be prepared to meet your God.
>
> All through the ages the prophets have looked down

through the corridors of time to our day. Billions of the deceased and those yet to be born have their eyes on us. Make no mistake about it—you are a marked generation. There has never been more expected of the faithful in such a short period of time as there is of us. Never before on the face of this earth have the forces of evil and the forces of good been as well organized. Now is the great day of the devil's power, with the greatest mass murderers of all time living among us. But now is also the great day of the Lord's power, with the greatest number ever of priesthood holders on the earth. And the showdown is fast approaching. ("In His Steps," in *Speeches of the Year, 1979* [Provo, Utah: BYU Press, 1980], p. 59)

There you have it—a prophet of God has described your mission to you. This is not the time for weak knees or faint hearts. The Lord has sent you to earth at this special time to participate in the great scenes preceding his second coming. Your life will not be easy before, during, or after your mission. Muscles are made strong through challenging the resistance of heavy weights. Spiritual muscles are strengthened by overcoming the resistance of heavy opposition.

You will never have another opportunity to serve as a single young man or woman. The more prepared you are when you arrive in your mission area, the more enjoyable your mission will be and the more success you will have. If you postpone preparing until you arrive, you will be cheating yourself and the Lord.

People from a million other worlds will want to talk to you about what it was like to serve a mission on this special world where their Savior worked out his infinite atonement. They will want to know how you were able to withstand the temptations and problems of a sin-sick world in the final days before wickedness was destroyed. They will want to hear a detailed account of the spiritual experiences you had and how you overcame the opposition you faced. If you have prepared with honor to serve with honor, you will be able to give a satisfactory report. Take advantage of the time remaining to prepare to go forth with honor.

INDEX